The Book On

Reinvention After Consequences

How to Start Over When the World Won't Stop Watching

The Book On Series

Rowan Blake

Published by The Book On Publishing, 2025.

First edition. September 14, 2025.

Website: https://thebookon.ca

Substack: https://thebookonpublishing.substack.com/

Reinvention After Consequences: How to Start Over When the World Won't Stop Watching

First edition. September 14, 2025.

Copyright © 2025 The Book On Publishing
ISBN: 978-1-997795-87-2

Written by Rowan Blake

Other Books in The Book On Series

Table of Contents

Read This First

This is not a book designed to entertain you. It's not here to charm, to soothe, or to hold your hand. It won't dazzle you with stories, metaphors, or motivational fluff. What you're having is a tool, an instruction manual written for people who are serious about learning, executing, and thinking at a higher level.

Every book in The Book On Series is built on a single premise: clarity beats complexity. We believe that when you strip away the noise, the emotions, the marketing spin, and the cultural rituals of "self-help," what's left is raw, unembellished instruction. That's what these books offer.

They are dry by design. Not because we don't care about language or narrative, but because when you're building something that matters, you don't need more distractions. You need a clear architecture. Mental scaffolding. Direction that respects your intelligence.

Each title in this series takes on a specific domain: decision-making, clarity, strategy, leverage, and uncertainty, and drills deep, not in sweeping generalizations, but in applied frameworks. These are books for builders, operators, founders, tacticians, and thinkers, people who don't just consume knowledge but operationalize it.

You'll find no chapter-long anecdotes here. No self-congratulatory memoirs. No bullet-point platitudes. Instead, what you'll get is structured insight: argument, example, application. The tone is direct. The prose is sober. The ideas are designed to be lifted out and used.

You won't be coddled, but you won't be misled either.

There's a place in the world for lyrical, emotional, story-driven books, and this isn't that place. This is a workspace. A blueprint. A conversation for people who are ready to act, not just absorb.

We respect your time and your intellect.

Welcome to The Book On Series

Part I: Losing the Old Self

Chapter 1: The Illusion of Stability

We like to imagine stability as a reward for surviving the chaos of youth, as if the right combination of money, relationships, and reputation will eventually stop the ground from shifting beneath our feet. I believed that for years, gripping the idea like driftwood. If I worked hard enough, proved myself enough, and pushed long enough, the world would settle.

For a while, it seemed to work. My days were full but predictable. There were deals to chase, bills to pay, and routines that felt almost ritualistic. I told myself this was maturity, that the wildness of my past was behind me, and I had earned something steady at last. People around me reinforced that story. They said things like "you've really made it through" or "things must finally feel solid." I let myself believe them because I wanted it to be true.

But stability isn't a fortress; it's an illusion. It's like walking on an ice sheet, smooth, glossy, reassuring, until you hear the snap beneath your boots and realize you've been living on something fragile all along. The cracks in my life had been spreading for years, but because they didn't announce themselves with explosions or drama, I ignored them. A shortcut here, a compromised value there, an argument smoothed over instead of resolved Each one was small enough to excuse. Added together, they were erosion.

I remember the metallic smell of that holding cell: disinfectant and old sweat. Collapse doesn't stay abstract when you feel it in your lungs. In that silence, I realized that reinvention doesn't begin with strategy; it starts with humiliation. The heaviest rubble is the ruin of self-image.

The collapse felt like betrayal. I had built that life brick by brick; how could it fall in one night? But it didn't. The collapse was years in the making. What I called stability had never been solid. The illusion comforts us, until it doesn't.

The lie of stability is seductive because it offers rest. It tells us we've crossed some invisible finish line, that we've arrived. After that, no more reinvention, no more upheaval, no more uncertainty. Just a steady plateau where nothing essential will change. But life doesn't care about our plateaus. A pink slip arrives after decades at the same company. A spouse who seemed permanent decides to leave. A body that felt immortal starts to betray us. The illusion comforts us right up until it doesn't.

History reminds us. The Titanic, declared unsinkable, was shattered by an iceberg. 2008's financial markets, propped up by denial, collapsed on millions. Nations fall. Empires dissolve. Stability is always temporary. But people forget, because believing in it helps us sleep.

When Berlin was divided after the war, families adapted to concrete walls cutting through their neighborhoods. Collapse forced them to reinvent daily rituals: walking miles to see a relative, smuggling notes, pretending the wall was not final even as it towered over them. That kind of communal improvisation mirrors the private improvisations we make after collapse: small, stubborn acts of survival that keep us human.

The illusion works hardest when you're closest to collapse. That was my blind spot. I convinced myself that I was beyond disaster precisely when the cracks were widening. It's not a coincidence. We cling hardest to the myth of permanence when the evidence against it is overwhelming. I wanted so badly to believe I had built something indestructible that I ignored every warning sign. The deals that made less and less sense, the erosion of trust in my marriage, the nagging voice in the back of my head that told me the shortcuts were adding up. I shoved it all down. Stability was the story I needed to say to myself.

Collapse strips more than possessions. It strips the illusion that you were ever in control. That was the deepest cut. I hadn't lost just my business or freedom; I lost my worldview. The belief that life could be project-managed into permanence.

And yet, collapse was clarifying. Once you see stability as a temporary arrangement, not a permanent reward, you stop being shocked when it fails. Collapse becomes less betrayal, more teacher.

Seneca warned centuries ago: Hold fortune lightly. The Buddha placed impermanence at the heart of truth. But modern culture resists this. We sell permanence. We package security. And when collapse comes, it feels personal, like a lie unraveling in public.

I once clung to a dead project, updating spreadsheets like rituals, pretending the collapse hadn't already happened. That's the paradox: collapse feels sudden, but it arrives long before we acknowledge it.

I don't buy it anymore. Stability was never the prize. It was the setup. The cracks were always there, waiting for the weight to spread them open. My collapse didn't reveal something new. It showed the truth that had been there all along.

The illusion of stability isn't just personal, it's cultural. Societies build myths of security. The Soviet Union promised care from cradle to grave, until it couldn't. Collapse wasn't just political, it was existential. When a system's story dies, so does the identity built on it.

The same happens quietly everywhere. A factory closes. A family business collapses. A stable routine evaporates. What felt like permanence was only a set of conditions that hadn't yet changed. But conditions always change.

Collapse shatters not just routines, but stories. Stories about who we are and what we can count on. Acknowledging instability threatens those stories, so we pretend, until we can't.

I remember the mental gymnastics I used to perform to protect the illusion. I'd tell myself the deals I was chasing were "just a rough patch" or that the compromises I made were "short-term adjustments." I'd say to myself the silence in a relationship was "normal" or that the unease I felt was simply stress from working hard. Each rationalization bought me more time, but what it really did was delay the reckoning. I wasn't protecting stability; I was defending an illusion with lies I told myself.

From Marcus Aurelius to the Buddha, the message is the same: clinging to permanence is suffering. Collapse forces that lesson. What Stoicism teaches in discipline, and Buddhism in release, collapse teaches in rubble.

People do this everywhere. A drinker insists they just need to cut back a little, right up until they're in rehab. An executive insists the numbers will rebound next quarter, right up until the board forces them out. A couple insists they're just going through a phase, right up until the divorce papers arrive. The illusion doesn't crack because of one event. It cracks because of years of denial layered into a fragile structure.

Ironically, collapse is often less painful than the years spent avoiding it. Naming the truth, however painful, is a relief. Collapse doesn't invent your pain. It exposes it.

This is why collapse, as brutal as it feels, is also clarifying. It forces honesty where there has been denial. It strips away the scaffolding of stories and leaves you staring at the bare frame of reality. It is humbling, humiliating, and often catastrophic, but it is real. And something is liberating, in fact, even when it hurts.

The danger is mistaking the illusion for reality, again. Survive one collapse, and rebuild the same lie in a new form. We crave safety, even if it's fiction. But pretending only delays the next fall.

Cultures that survive collapse best are those that accept impermanence. In Japan, homes are built to be rebuilt. In parts of Africa, identity lives in rituals that outlast buildings. In Buddhist tradition, monks meditate on death, not to fear it, but to remember what passes.

Katrina showed collapse at scale. Survivors improvised a community, carved out resilience, and adapted. Collapse separates those who improvise meaning from those who wait for rescue.

In the modern West, we're sold forever: forever homes, forever pensions, forever love. When reality intrudes, we don't just grieve the loss; we grieve the myth we built on it.

What I lost wasn't just freedom or success. It was a framework. A belief that life could be controlled. The collapse exposed how fragile that belief had always been.

Sitting in that cell, I saw the man I'd been pretending to be fall away. I hated what was left. But what was left as real.

He wasn't a fraud. He was what had been hiding under the mask of certainty.

Collapse removes masks. It reveals what was always fragile. It is not betrayal, it is truth. Painful, humbling truth.

Living with that truth is the challenge. It's tempting to rebuild the illusion. But the work is to remain awake, even when it hurts.

I once believed that the collapse ended meaning. Now I know it reveals it. Collapse strips illusion so meaning can be rebuilt, not from fantasy, but from truth.

That doesn't mean living in fear. It means living awake. It means not mistaking quiet seas for safety or strong walls for permanence. It means knowing that everything can shift, and when it does, it's not a betrayal, it's just reality reminding you of what you forgot.

What I came to understand, slowly and painfully, is that the illusion of stability is not just a misunderstanding. It is a form of addiction. Once you've had a taste of it, you want more. You crave the sense that things will hold, that the story you're living won't be interrupted. You bargain with yourself to keep it going. You ignore red flags, silence doubts, and shut your eyes to the cracks widening beneath your feet. You convince yourself that if you just try harder, you can make the illusion real.

I see it everywhere now. I see it in friends who hate their jobs but cling to the paycheck because it feels safer than the unknown. I see it in couples who haven't spoken honestly in years but still wear rings because divorce would destroy the illusion of permanence. I see it in politicians who cling to power long after their legitimacy has evaporated, hoping the trappings of office will hold off collapse a little longer. What we call responsibility is often just fear of losing the illusion.

It's not entirely our fault. We are taught to chase stability from the start. Parents, teachers, bosses, everyone says the same thing: find something solid and hold onto it. We measure lives in terms of stability: a stable job, a stable family, a stable retirement plan. Nobody celebrates instability. Nobody encourages young people to prepare for collapse as an inevitability. We build entire educational systems, financial systems, and even religious systems on the promise that permanence is achievable if you follow the rules. Collapse is treated like an aberration, not the norm.

But the truth is the opposite. Collapse is the rule. Stability is the exception. Civilizations rise and fall. Companies expand and implode. Bodies thrive and then decay. Relationships blossom and then wither. To expect permanence is like expecting summer to last forever. It's not just naïve, it's dangerous. Because when winter comes, it's not the cold that kills you. It's your refusal to accept that the season has changed.

When I lost everything, I thought the hardest part would be rebuilding. But it wasn't. The hardest part was grieving the loss of the illusion itself. I had built my life around the promise that stability was possible, that once I had it, I could relax. When that illusion shattered, I felt like I had lost not just a life, but a worldview. It was as if someone had erased the map I'd been using to navigate. For months, I wandered through shame, confusion, and bitterness, trying to find another story that would reassure me. Eventually, I stopped looking. I realized there was no new illusion to replace the old one. There was only the truth: life is fragile, unstable, and uncontrollable.

That realization sounds bleak at first. People recoil from it, the way they recoil from hearing about death. They want reassurance, not honesty. But I've found that once you stop resisting it, impermanence becomes liberating. If nothing is permanent, then failure isn't final. If stability is always temporary, then collapse is not the end; it's just part of the rhythm. If control is an illusion, then letting go isn't weakness, it's sanity.

The great mistake of my earlier life was not that I collapsed, but that I believed collapse could never happen. That belief blinded me. It made me arrogant, careless, and deaf to the warnings. Collapse didn't betray me. My illusion did.

When you really absorb that, it changes how you live. You stop chasing security at all costs. You stop clinging to jobs, relationships, or reputations that are already cracking. You stop measuring yourself by how steady things look from the outside. You begin to value resilience over stability, adaptability over control. You start asking not "how do I hold this forever?" but "how do I respond when this changes?" That shift is the beginning of reinvention.

I sometimes wonder what my life would have looked like if I'd learned that lesson earlier. Could I have avoided collapse altogether? Maybe. But probably not. The illusion is too seductive, and most people don't abandon it until they're forced to. It takes the shock of reality, the pink slip, the divorce decree, the diagnosis, the handcuffs, for us to wake up. Until then, we hold onto the myth because it makes us feel safe. That's the irony: the very thing that comforts us is what makes collapse more devastating when it comes.

Now, when I look at people still living inside the illusion, I don't feel judgment. I feel recognition. I see my old self, the one who thought he had finally arrived, the one who mistook routines for permanence, the one who couldn't imagine the cracks widening into a chasm. I want to tell them the truth, but I know they won't hear it until they have to. That's how the illusion works. It holds until it breaks.

And yet, I also know this: once you've seen through the illusion, you can never fully go back. You might still crave stability. You might still chase it sometimes. But in the back of your mind, you'll hear the ice cracking. You'll know better. And that knowledge, painful as it is, is also the seed of freedom.

The strange gift of collapse is that it strips away the one lie that runs deepest: the belief that stability is real. Once that lie is gone, you begin to live differently. You stop assuming tomorrow will look like today. You stop bargaining with permanence. You start to measure your life not by how stable it seems, but by how well you adapt when stability breaks apart.

This is not the same as cynicism. Cynicism says nothing matters because everything ends. Honesty says everything ends, so what you do while it lasts matters even more. If a job isn't forever, then how you show up in it today matters more. If love can dissolve, then the way you treat someone in this moment carries even greater weight. If your health will eventually falter, then the decision to care for your body right now has meaning even though it won't guarantee immortality. Impermanence makes each choice sharper.

When I stopped pretending stability was guaranteed, I began to notice how much energy I had wasted trying to defend it. I had poured time, money, and pride into propping up facades that were destined to fall anyway. I tried to impress people who would eventually vanish from my life. I tried to shore up businesses that were built on foundations already cracked. I tried to hold onto relationships long after trust had evaporated. All of it was wasted effort because none of it could survive the forces of change. What I could have done instead, and what I do now, is direct that energy toward building resilience. Toward learning skills that can survive multiple collapses.

Toward cultivating friendships that endure not because they're convenient but because they're tested. Toward practices that steady me when everything else shakes.

That shift changes the way you face the world. Instead of asking, "How can I make this stable forever?" you begin to ask, "What will help me stand when this shifts?" That second question is honest. It prepares you not just for survival, but for reinvention. Because reinvention is not what you do after collapse, it is what you do when you accept that collapse is part of the deal.

The illusion of stability doesn't die easily. Even now, after everything, I sometimes catch myself wishing for it. Wishing I could go back to the days when I thought permanence was possible, when I thought the ice under my feet would never crack. But then I remember what those days really felt like: tense, anxious, desperate to maintain the mask. I don't want that back. I'd rather live with instability than with denial. I'd rather live awake, even when it hurts, than sleepwalk through another illusion.

That's why this book begins here. Before we talk about reinvention, we have to face the truth about collapse. Before we talk about rebuilding, we have to admit what was never truly stable in the first place. If you can't let go of the illusion, you can't truly begin again. You'll only repeat the same cycle, building the same fragile structures, telling yourself the same comforting lies. The first step is honesty: stability was never real. The second step is courage: live anyway.

I used to think collapse was the end of everything. Now I think of it as the beginning of honesty. Once you've faced it, you stop being surprised when things fall apart. You stop being betrayed by impermanence. You start to live as if the cracks are always spreading, because they are. And somehow, that makes life richer. Not safer, not easier, but truer. And truth, even when it burns, is a better foundation than illusion ever was.

Before you begin the following exercise, take a moment. Breathe. This isn't about fear; it's about facing truth now, so it doesn't ambush you later.

Chapter 1 Exercise: Inventory Your Illusions

Write down five things in your life you consider stable: your job, relationship, finances, health, and reputation. Then ask: What if this disappeared tomorrow? Who would I be without it?

Let your discomfort guide you. That discomfort is the sound of illusions cracking. Sit with it.

Finish by writing this statement and saying it aloud:

"Stability is not guaranteed. Collapse is part of life. My task is not to avoid it, but to live awake inside it."

Chapter 2: The Fall Nobody Plans For

If collapse came with a countdown clock, we'd all be wiser. Red lights flashing above our heads might prompt different choices. But collapse doesn't work that way. It hides inside ordinary days, wearing the mask of normal life, until it takes everything in one decisive blow.

The fall nobody plans for feels impossible—right up until it happens. One day, you're living your familiar story. Next, you're a character in a cautionary tale. A headline. A whisper. And the thought you can't shake is: this can't be my life.

In the first week after my collapse, I moved like a ghost through rooms that no longer knew me. Nothing had shifted physically, but everything had changed. Even the chipped mug in the sink felt like a relic of a person who was gone.

Looking back, the warnings were obvious—long nights chasing flimsy opportunities. Compromises hardened into habits. The silence in my marriage, the gut-level unease I ignored. Each crack was dismissed as temporary. The foundation was failing, and I was the last to admit it.

Collapse isn't cinematic. It's paperwork, handcuffs, fluorescent lights: no violins, no drama, just a system catching up with your denial. I didn't feel anger. I felt disbelief. How could something that seemed permanent vanish so fast?

Psychologists call it identity collapse, the loss not just of what you had, but who you believed yourself to be. A soldier was discharged. An athlete retired. A spouse has divorced. The structures vanish, but the deeper loss is of self-concept. That's what makes collapse so disorienting.

I thought I was competent, resilient, strategic, someone who bent the world to his will. But collapse exposes the gap between the story you told and the reality you face. Sitting in that cell, none of those labels applied. I wasn't a leader. I wasn't strong. I was powerless and ashamed.

After the Soviet Union fell, grocery shelves were empty, jobs vanished overnight, and families stared into silence. What seemed like chaos from outside was, for them, a hollowing out. Collapse doesn't always explode. Sometimes it just... vanishes.

History repeats the lesson: Napoleon in exile. Nixon in disgrace. Giants reduced to shadows. Blockbuster. Kodak.

BlackBerry. Once unshakable, then obsolete. Collapse arrives for emperors and executives alike.

The hardest part is that even as collapse unfolds, we deny it. I did. I repeated: This can't be happening as if my disbelief might pause reality. Denial is not resistance. It's paralysis.

The fall nobody plans for comes for everyone. A call from a doctor. A foreclosure notice. A betrayal. A scandal. The details differ. The feeling is the same: disorientation, disbelief, the sudden death of your story.

That is collapse in its truest form. Not just the loss of things, but the loss of the narrative that told you who you were. That's why it feels impossible to plan for. We can prepare for setbacks, even disasters. But planning for the death of a story? That's a different kind of impossibility. And yet, it happens to everyone. The question is never if. It is only when.

I tried to outrun silence, with noise, busyness, and distraction. But silence doesn't shrink. It waits. Only in stillness did I realize silence wasn't the enemy. It was the teacher.

Collapse looks ordinary from the outside. You see someone making poor decisions and say, 'They should've known.' But when it's your life, you're too close to see the frame. What looks like a rough patch is often the beginning of the end.

I remember the numbness, unanswered calls, unread texts, and the looks of people who didn't know what to say. That silence confirms it: things are different now. You're different now. And they can't unsee it.

But collapse is internal too—the self fractures. You interrogate every choice, rerun the timeline, and imagine alternate outcomes. It's a haunting, not by ghosts, but by the version of yourself that never fell.

Philosophers call it liminal space, the threshold between identities. The old self gone, the new one unnamed. Collapse drops you there with no guide, no map, just the wreckage.

No amount of reflection undoes collapse. The old identity is gone. And that's what separates collapse from mere failure: it ends the story you were in.

When I finally began to emerge from the initial shock, I realized how much denial had shaped me. I had been living in a story so fragile that it required constant self-deception to keep it going. The late nights, the compromises, the justifications, they were all small acts of denial, and I mistook them for resilience. But resilience is facing reality and adapting to it. What I was practicing was avoidance, and avoidance only makes collapse sharper when it arrives.

Collapse doesn't just destroy, it makes you doubt your ability to build again. After my fall, I didn't even trust myself to buy cereal. If I could ruin my life, what made me think I could choose breakfast?

But here's the paradox: collapse clears away the illusions you refused to release. Without it, you'd keep pretending. Collapse is a brutal purge, but it makes truth possible.

Everyone has a version. A man betrayed. A business lost. A diagnosis that resets everything. The outside changes are real, but the real collapse is internal: the story dies.

After Japan's 2011 tsunami, there were nights when no one spoke. But in that quiet, people began to move, breathe, and endure. Collapse teaches community first through silence, then through survival.

Collapse feels final. But it isn't. It clears the illusion, forces you into reality. Not the end of the story, just the end of pretending.

I didn't see the possibility right away. At first, all I saw was ruin. But over time, I saw what was left: the part of me that wasn't built on illusion.

Collapse strips away fantasy. What remains is the only place where you can build something real.

The days after the collapse feel like a suspension of time. The world outside moves forward, but for you, everything has stopped. Friends go to work, neighbors mow their lawns, and the news keeps reporting on everything but your disaster. You sit in the ruins of your own life, watching everyone else carry on, and wonder how it's possible that the world didn't notice the earthquake that flattened you. That sense of dissonance is part of the cruelty of collapse. You are undone while the world is unchanged.

I had to learn to hear silence not as absence but as instruction. It showed me what had been hollow all along. It stripped away the busy armor I wore to convince myself I mattered. In that bareness, I glimpsed something harder than collapse itself: the possibility of beginning without illusions.

I used to think collapse would make me stronger instantly, the way stories and films make it seem. A man loses everything, suffers, and emerges with clarity and grit. The reality is different. Collapse does not immediately teach. It scrapes you raw. It breaks the skin and leaves you open to infection. You don't wake up with resilience. You wake up with shame and fear. Strength is not the gift collapse gives you automatically; it is the possibility collapse offers if you survive it. And survival is not guaranteed.

Some people never rebuild. I've seen it. A man fired late in his career who never finds meaningful work again. A woman who loses a child and spends the rest of her life in bitterness. A family wiped out by debt that never crawls out of the shadow of that humiliation. Collapse does not come with a promise of reinvention. It comes with an invitation, and the invitation can be refused. That is what terrified me most in the beginning: the sense that I might stay stuck in the rubble forever, that this new broken self was permanent, that the story had ended here.

What begins to shift is not some sudden insight but the tiniest flicker of possibility. You realize that you woke up another day. You understand that collapse didn't kill you, though it felt like it should have. You know that if you are still here, you might as well move, if only an inch. It is not a burst of hope, but a reluctant step. And that reluctant step is the beginning of reinvention.

Looking back, I see that my collapse was inevitable. Not because of fate or destiny, but because of the way I had been living. I ignored cracks, I believed illusions, I chose shortcuts. Collapse wasn't a freak accident; it was the bill coming due. The same is true for most people. They believe they were ambushed, but when they look closely, they see the pattern. The betrayals ignored, the debts piled up, the warnings shrugged off. Collapse is rarely sudden. It is a gradual erosion revealed all at once.

Collapse feels like the end. But really, it's the chapter you wouldn't end yourself, so life ends it for you.

Collapse is the most honest teacher you'll ever meet. It doesn't flatter. It doesn't spare you. It leaves you raw and ready, if you survive it.

The fall nobody plans for comes for everyone. A call from a doctor. A foreclosure notice. A betrayal. A scandal. The details differ. The feeling is the same: disorientation, disbelief, the sudden death of your story.

Before you begin this exercise, take a deep breath. This is not an academic task. It's an emotional reckoning, and a path to freedom.

Chapter 2 Exercise: Failure Autopsy

Write out the story of your last collapse in painful, specific detail. Who was there? What happened? What did you lose? How did it feel?

Underline every warning sign. Every ignored truth. Every pattern repeated. These are not just memories. They are evidence.

Now list those patterns. Don't judge. Just name them. Where are they still active in you today?

Finish by writing:

"Collapse is not sudden. It is built. If I can name the patterns, I can break them."

Chapter 3: Public Failure vs Private Shame

There are two kinds of collapse. One happens in the quiet corners of your life, whispered behind closed doors, invisible to most of the world. The other occurs in the open, where everyone you know can see it, where strangers form opinions about you without knowing your name, where the failure is not just lived but displayed. I've lived both, and I can tell you: private collapse wounds the soul, but public collapse devours the dignity.

When failure is public, you are reduced to a headline. The complexity of your story is erased and flattened into a single word: fraud, addict, bankrupt, criminal. People who know nothing about you feel entitled to pass judgment. Neighbors whisper, former friends keep their distance, strangers on the internet sharpen their knives. Public shame is a bonfire, and you are the fuel.

I still remember the feeling of seeing my own name in print, stripped of nuance, reduced to a caricature. The story wasn't wrong, not exactly. It was just incomplete. It was the most damning version of the truth, polished for easy consumption. In the eyes of the world, I was no longer a husband, a father, an entrepreneur, a man who had tried and failed and stumbled. I was a criminal. That one word swallowed all the others.

History is full of public shaming that became cautionary tales. The Salem witch trials reduced women to archetypes: hysteric, liar, threat, while the reality of their lives was erased. The brutality was not only in the executions but in the way complexity was flattened into caricature. This is the same violence of headlines: the transformation of human beings into symbols.

But the brutality of public collapse doesn't end with the judgment of others. What follows is the quieter corrosion of private shame. When the headlines fade, when the neighbors stop talking, when the strangers move on to the next scandal, you are left alone with yourself. And the silence is worse. Public failure humiliates you in front of the world. Private shame whispers that the world was right. That you are nothing but the worst thing you ever did.

Private shame is relentless because it speaks in your own voice. You replay conversations with people who trusted you. You imagine their disappointment. You hear the venom of your own self-condemnation. And unlike the headlines, which eventually move to the back of the paper, your shame is always breaking news inside your head. It tells you that no matter what you do, no matter how long you live, you will never outgrow the moment of your disgrace.

What makes shame so corrosive is not just its persistence, but its intimacy. You can shrug off the judgment of strangers. You can even resist the coldness of acquaintances. But when the shame is coming from inside you, there is no escape. Every silence feels like condemnation. Every glance feels like an accusation. Even kindness feels contaminated, as if people are only being nice because they pity you.

Cultures treat shame differently, but the weight is the same. In Western societies, shame is often framed as individual: you did wrong, you bear the burden. In many Eastern cultures, shame is collective; the disgrace stains not just you, but your family, your community, and your ancestors. Both are crushing in their own way. In one, you feel isolated beyond redemption. In the other, you feel like you've dragged everyone you love into the mud with you. Either way, shame is exile.

And yet, public failure and private shame are not the same thing. Public failure is an event. Private shame is a process. One ends quickly; the other lingers for years. I thought once the trial was over, once the headlines moved on, I would begin to feel relief. I was wrong. That's when the real collapse began, because that's when I had to live with myself.

Public collapse taught me how merciless the world can be. Private shame taught me how merciless I could be to myself. And the latter is far harder to escape.

What I didn't understand at first was how shame rewires your perception of the world. After my collapse, I could walk into a grocery store and feel like every set of eyes was on me, even if no one knew who I was. Shame distorts your vision. It convinces you that everyone is watching, everyone is judging, even when in reality, most people are too absorbed in their own lives to care. But that doesn't matter, because shame lives in your skin. You project it onto every glance, every silence, every interaction.

I remember standing in line at a coffee shop, hearing two people whisper behind me, and being certain they were talking about me. They weren't. But shame made it impossible to believe otherwise. That's the thing about shame: once it takes root, you no longer need other people to condemn you. You do it for them. You carry the jury inside your chest.

The Japanese concept of *haji*, shame, captures this same weight. In that cultural frame, your disgrace is not yours alone; it stains ancestors and descendants alike. That burden can feel unbearable, but it also reveals shame's universality. No culture escapes it. Only the terms differ.

At night, shame grows even louder. You replay everything. You run endless loops of what you did, what you should have done, what you should have said. You construct elaborate fantasies where you make different choices, where you walk away before the damage, where you stop yourself from stepping over the line. The mind becomes a torture chamber, inventing infinite variations of the past that will never exist. That's why private shame is often worse than public humiliation. The public moves on. You don't.

In some ways, I think shame is a survival mechanism. The mind attempts to keep us from repeating the same mistakes. Painful memory etched so deeply that it can't be ignored. The problem is, shame doesn't stay in its lane. It doesn't just remind you of what you did wrong. It convinces you that wrong is all you are. The act becomes the identity. That's the trap. And once you accept that trap, rebuilding feels impossible. Why try to build on a foundation that you believe is already poisoned?

History is full of people who carried shame as a permanent weight. Some never escaped it. Others turned it into fuel. Martha Stewart went from being a punchline after prison to becoming, improbably, a cultural icon again. Her crime didn't vanish, but she refused to let shame be the last chapter. Nelson Mandela spent twenty-seven years in prison, but when he walked free, he refused to let shame or bitterness define him. He transformed it into authority and moral weight. These are rare examples, but they prove shame can be metabolized into something else.

Most of us are not Martha Stewart or Mandela. Most of us carry our shame quietly, hoping no one notices, hoping it fades on its own. It doesn't. Shame does not dissolve with time. If left alone, it hardens. It becomes part of your identity, a lens through which you see everything. That's why people years removed from their collapse still speak in the language of disgrace. "I'm the guy who ruined his marriage." "I'm the woman who bankrupted her business." "I'm the one who got caught." Shame keeps your worst moment alive indefinitely.

The cruelest part is how it seeps into your relationships. People may forgive you, but shame won't allow you to believe them. You keep waiting for the moment when their kindness wears off, when their patience snaps, when their hidden resentment surfaces. So you hold back. You don't fully trust their acceptance, because you don't fully accept yourself. Shame turns even love into suspicion.

The other cruelty is how it turns your own future into a shadow. Opportunities come, and you hesitate. You tell yourself you don't deserve them. You imagine what people would say if they knew the truth. You self-sabotage because you believe you're still living under the verdict of the past. Shame convinces you that collapse wasn't just an event, but a permanent condition.

The philosopher Kierkegaard described despair as the sickness unto death: the belief that you can never be anything other than your worst moment. Reading that later, I realized he was describing what shame had already done to me. It is philosophy written in flesh and memory.

I know this because I lived it for years. I thought I had served my time, paid my price, faced my collapse. But the deeper sentence was the one I carried inside, long after the legal one had ended. I sentenced myself to years of shame, years of silence, years of believing that nothing I did could outweigh the worst thing I had done. And the tragedy is that nobody was holding me there but me.

The turning point didn't come all at once. It never does. It came in moments, someone I thought would despise me offering an unexpected kindness, a conversation where someone acknowledged my past but didn't treat me as if I was still stuck in it, a day when I managed to go an hour, then a day, without rehearsing the old shame script. Little breaks in the pattern. Tiny cracks of light. And eventually, the realization that shame is not truth. It is a story. And like all stories, it can be rewritten.

But before that realization comes, shame feels like gravity. It holds you down, pulls you inward, and convinces you that you will never stand again. Public failure may make you fall, but private shame convinces you that you don't deserve to rise. And that is the greater danger, because collapse is survivable, but living forever inside shame is not truly living at all.

The hardest lesson I've learned is that shame has no natural endpoint. Failure has consequences, punishment has an expiration date, but shame will outlast both if you let it. The law can release you. Debt can be repaid. Even relationships can be repaired or replaced. But shame is a self-renewing sentence, and only you can decide when it ends. That's what makes it so dangerous. It can keep you imprisoned long after the walls around you have opened.

At first, I thought time itself would cure me. I believed that if I stayed quiet, kept my head down, and let the years pass, shame would soften. It didn't. Time only made it more insidious. It dug deeper grooves in my mind, until every thought seemed to run downhill toward guilt and regret. The silence of shame is deceptive that way. You think it's receding, but really it's rooting itself more firmly inside you.

It took me a long time to see that shame was not a sentence handed down by the world. It was a story I was telling myself, a verdict I had chosen to accept. That doesn't mean the world is merciful. Some people will never see me as anything but the sum of my worst actions. Some people will always flatten me into a headline, always whisper behind my back, always define me by the collapse. But their voices are not the problem. The problem is when I make their voices my own.

That is the distinction between public failure and private shame. Public failure is what they say about you. Private shame is what you say about yourself. The first thing you can't control. The second, eventually, you can. And the strange thing is that once you shift the second, the first begins to matter less. When you stop living under your own condemnation, the condemnation of others loses its power. They may still whisper. They may still judge. But it no longer dictates who you are.

This shift doesn't happen through denial. It doesn't come from pretending you didn't collapse or that the damage wasn't real. Lies don't defeat shame. It is defeated by honesty. By admitting, without flinching, what you did, what it cost, who it hurt, and then refusing to accept that this is the only story left to tell. That is not denial. That is reinvention. And reinvention begins with the audacity to say: I am more than my worst moment.

The world resists this. We live in a culture that loves permanent labels—once disgraced, always disgraced. Once broken, always broken. We cling to the myth that people never change because it makes us feel safer. If they are doomed to remain what they were, then we don't have to wrestle with the uncomfortable possibility that we might change, too. But history, experience, and human resilience all tell a different story. People do change. People rebuild. People reinvent. The evidence is everywhere if you're willing to look past the headlines.

I know this because I've lived it. I spent years believing shame was the whole story, only to realize it was one chapter. Painful, humiliating, unforgettable, but not final. When I began to act differently, when I started to rebuild even in small ways, I discovered that shame is allergic to movement. It thrives in paralysis. It withers in action. Every step forward is a small defiance of shame's gravity. Every act of honesty, every choice to show up again, every refusal to hide is a declaration that shame will not dictate the rest of your life.

Oscar Wilde knew this truth. When he was imprisoned for 'gross indecency,' he became a tabloid spectacle. But in his writings from prison, he spoke of shame as a crucible, a place where illusions were stripped away. His work reminds us that shame does not just break, it also refines, if we refuse to let it reduce us to ash.

Public failure doesn't vanish. Private shame doesn't disappear overnight. They remain as shadows, reminders of what was lost. But they don't have to be the whole picture. They can be context instead of destiny. That's the distinction that makes reinvention possible. Without it, collapse becomes a life sentence. With it, collapse becomes the harsh beginning of something truer.

Chapter 3 Exercise: Public vs Private

This exercise is designed to help you separate the two forces that collapse unleashes, the judgment of the world and the judgment of yourself. They feel like the same weight, but they are not. One you cannot control. The other you can.

Write two versions of your collapse story. The first is the public version, the one told about you, the version flattened into gossip or headlines or reputation. Write it as if you were a stranger, summarizing the collapse in the bluntest, least sympathetic way possible. Don't soften it. This is the story the world sees.

Now write the private version, the one only you know—the messy details, the context, the fears, the motives, the regrets, the humanity. Write the story that never makes it into the headlines.

When you're done, compare the two. Notice the gap. The first is incomplete, and the second is uncomfortable. Both are real, but neither is the whole truth.

Underneath both versions, write one more sentence: I am not either of these stories. I am the person who lived them, and I am still living.

Modern culture has its own theatre of shame: social media. A single mistake can become permanent digital evidence, shared, memed, and replayed without context. The cruelty is that the punishment outlives the act.

Reinvention in this world requires not only private defiance but public stamina, choosing to live again in sight of the mob.

This is not about absolving yourself. It's about refusing to let the world or your shame write the last line of your story. The worst thing you did is part of you. The disgrace that followed is part of you. But neither defines you completely, unless you decide they do.

Chapter 4: The Weight of Judgment

Judgment is heavier than iron. You can serve a sentence, wear the cuffs, endure the fallout; those things have an end date. Judgment doesn't. It lingers like smoke that never clears. It sits in the room with you, follows you into the grocery store, and clings to your name when someone says it. It looks back at you in the mirror. Judgment is invisible, but you feel its pressure every hour you're awake.

After my collapse, I couldn't walk into a store without thinking every glance was loaded, every silence in the checkout line a verdict. No one said anything. They didn't have to. Judgment rarely shouts; it whispers just loud enough for you to fill in the blanks yourself. A neighbor's wave feels too stiff. A friend paused too long. A smile doesn't reach the eyes, and suddenly it's proof. You tell yourself it's paranoia, but deep down you know some of it is real. The world does judge. The question is whether you let its voice drown out your own.

For a long time, I thought judgment was purely external, inflicted on me by other people. But the worst judgment came from inside. I became my own prosecutor, jury, and executioner. Every memory of failure was dragged into an imaginary courtroom where I lost the case over and over again. Even kindness from others became suspect. I told myself they didn't mean it, that compassion was pity, that anyone willing to forgive must not know the whole story. The outside world might eventually move on. My own judgment refused to.

That is why collapse is so hard to outlive. You can rebuild a career, repair relationships, even regain a reputation, but if you keep dragging judgment around in your head, you never truly leave the wreckage. You can sentence yourself to a lifetime of invisible punishment long after everyone else has forgotten the crime.

Cultures have always known how to weaponize this. In small villages, exile could be worse than death, a permanent mark that you were cast out. Religion has used judgment as a shadow to keep human impulses in line. Now technology has turned judgment into a public archive that never fades. Screenshots, headlines, search results, your worst moment becomes a permanent Exhibit A. The medieval scarlet letter used to be sewn to your clothing. Today, it's sewn into your digital footprint.

But here's the thing: judgment, while crushing, can also be reshaped. I learned that the only way to keep moving was to stop waiting for permission. The judgment of others didn't disappear. It just stopped being the steering wheel of my life. Slowly, the actions of my days grew louder than the whispers. Consistency became a kind of rebuttal. People who once doubted began to notice effort where there had been denial, honesty where there had been excuses. Judgment lost some of its hold.

This doesn't mean judgment vanishes. It never does. Some people will never forgive, never forget, never let you be more than your worst moment. But their voices don't have to be the loudest in the room. The real battle is not silencing the world; it's silencing the echo chamber inside yourself. Once you do that, judgment becomes background noise. Still there, but no longer the soundtrack of your life.

When you live under judgment, you shrink. You censor yourself, stop taking risks, and avoid places where you might be seen. You disappear from your own story piece by piece. That's the true danger: not that people judge you, but that you begin to live as if their judgment is destiny. Most of the time, people aren't thinking about you nearly as much as you think they are. But once your brain has been rewired by collapse, you expect condemnation everywhere, and in expecting it, you act as if it's already happening.

I've watched people destroy themselves not because of the collapse, but because of judgment. A man loses a job, could recover, but never applies again because he assumes everyone will see him as damaged goods. A woman survives divorce but hides for years, convinced everyone views her as broken. The event was survivable. The story they told themselves afterward was not.

This is what sociologists call labeling theory. Once you're branded, the label becomes your identity, and you start living up to it. That's what makes judgment so dangerous: it doesn't just punish; it reshapes who you think you are. If you believe the label long enough, it becomes prophecy.

But judgment can be turned into raw material. Once you stop trying to outrun it, you can carry it differently. It becomes ballast. Heavy, yes, but stabilizing. If you stop burning energy on erasing judgment, you can spend that energy on living in a way that outlasts it. You stop arguing with the world about who you are and start proving it with what you do.

That shift changes everything. People may still whisper, but your consistency drowns out their whispers. Actions outlive rumor. Effort outlives accusation. And judgment, while never fully gone, becomes something you can walk with instead of something that pins you to the ground.

There is dignity in this. Not defiance, not pretending you don't care, but quiet resolve: I will live well even if forgiveness never comes. I will build under the weight. That's how judgment stops crushing you and starts grounding you. And the truth is, most of the judgment you fear is your own reflection. The day you forgive yourself, not excuse, not forget, but forgive, is the day the outside voices finally lose their power.

Chapter 4 Exercise: Voices Audit

Ancient Rome had *damnatio memoriae*, the condemnation of memory. Your name was chiseled off monuments, your face erased from coins. Modern judgment is less formal but works the same way: it tries to convince you that you deserve to be erased. This exercise is a way of refusing that sentence.

Take a sheet of paper and draw two columns:

Label one "External Voices", write down the judgments you've heard or believe others carry about you. Be specific.

Label the other "Internal Voices", write the accusations you say to yourself at three in the morning, the words only you can hear.

When you're done, rank each voice by how much power it has over you. Which ones shape your decisions the most? Which ones stop you from trying?

Now, circle the voices you would ignore if you believed you had nothing left to prove. Sit with that question: *What would my life look like if I stopped obeying these voices?*

This is not about silencing judgment. You can't. It's about separating what belongs to others from what belongs to you, and then deciding which voices get to speak into your future. Over time, the consistency of your actions will weigh more than rumor, and that weight will be proof.

Part II: The Work of Rebuilding

Chapter 5: Clearing the Rubble

Reinvention never begins the way people like to picture it. Everyone loves the phoenix story: you crash, you burn, you rise, wings blazing, stronger than ever. It's cinematic. It's comforting. It's also fiction. Reinvention doesn't start in firelight; it begins on your knees, in the dirt, staring at the mess of what used to be your life and realizing you can't glue it back together.

After my collapse, I tried anyway. I told myself the cracks could be smoothed, the shards reassembled. I worked to convince the world nothing had really changed, that I could patch over the damage and make everyone forget. That's what denial does: it promises restoration. But rubble is not repairable. Once the walls fall, there is no going back. The only honest step forward is admitting the structure is gone and clearing the ground where it stood.

Those first mornings were the worst. I would sit at the same kitchen table, stare at the unpaid bills scattered across it like an indictment, and feel the air in the room pressing down like judgment. Nothing had moved, but nothing belonged to me anymore. That's what rubble feels like: familiar surroundings haunted by the absence of what they once meant.

Clearing the rubble isn't housekeeping. It's grieving with your eyes open. Collapse leaves behind ghosts, people you loved, dreams you built, versions of yourself you once believed in. They remain in fragments, tempting you to hold them, convincing you that if you grip hard enough, you can make them whole again. But ghosts do not rebuild. They keep you frozen.

I had a single box by my door that became my shrine to the past: a badge, a lanyard, some handwritten notes from colleagues. I told myself they were harmless keepsakes. They weren't. They were anchors. In the morning, I emptied that box, I sat on the floor and read every piece. I didn't rage, didn't cry, didn't perform forgiveness. I simply admitted aloud: the person who earned these is gone. That moment wasn't closure; it was the beginning of an honest inventory.

I've seen people refuse to do this work for years. They keep the job long after it has turned to dust because quitting would mean admitting the career has ended. They stay in a marriage long past its prime because leaving would mean facing the loneliness waiting underneath. They keep wearing the mask of success because dropping it would mean confronting the question of who they really are without it. These are the ruins we squat in, hoping the walls will rise by magic. They never do.

Communities, ironically, handle collapse better than most individuals. After a natural disaster, after war, after the unthinkable, someone eventually picks up a sledgehammer to finish what the destruction started. New Orleans learned this after Katrina. Christchurch, New Zealand, realized it after its earthquakes. The work of rebuilding began not with blueprints but with organized clearing. Bucket brigades. Bulldozers. Volunteers who knew that mourning was not enough, the ruins had to go.

Personal collapse is the same. You must become your own demolition crew, your own inspector, your own zoning board. You must name what is beyond saving and remove it before anything new can stand. This feels merciless at first, like rubbing salt in a wound. But naming what is gone is the first act of mercy you can give yourself.

I clung to fantasies for a long time, telling myself I could fix everything if I just tried hard enough. Every time I revisited the wreckage, I rearranged it into a pattern that looked like my past life. And every time, the pieces refused. They weren't alive; they were remains. The sooner you accept that, the sooner you can start again.

Clearing rubble is brutal, yes, but it is the only way to uncover open ground. At first, that emptiness feels terrifying, barren, exposed, like standing in the middle of nowhere with no map. But over time, you see that open ground is a possibility. Nothing can be built on denial. Anything can be built on cleared space.

What makes clearing so hard is how seductive rubble can be. It's proof that something once existed. The shards of a marriage remind you that once, love was alive. The papers from a failed business remind you that once, ambition burned hot. Even the ruins of reputation whisper that once, you were somebody else. You keep them because they comfort you, but really, they are holding you.

I did this too. For months, I kept documents, emails, and objects that let me pretend the past was recoverable. I would sit among them and replay scenes, rewrite outcomes, bargain with ghosts. It was a time machine, and I used it nightly. But time machines don't rebuild houses. They only trap you in loops.

Rubble can be mental as much as physical. You can throw away the papers, sell the house, cut ties with people, and still wake up living inside the ruins in your head. Shame is rubble. Regret is rubble. The habits that led you here are rubble. Clearing means dismantling those, too, naming the memories that still sting, the voices you still obey, the patterns you still repeat.

I had to clear my calendar before I could clear my head. Cancel meetings that existed only to preserve an image, archive conversations that had become mausoleums, and write one blunt email that simply said: I am ending this. Thank you. Goodbye.

I'll never forget a friend who came by, looked around at the chaos in my living room, and said quietly, "You know none of this is coming back, right?" I wanted to argue, but I couldn't. The mess wasn't evidence of something waiting to be restored. It was evidence of a life that had ended.

Communities after earthquakes understand this faster than we do about our own lives. They grieve, but they dig. They know the rubble is dangerous, that leaving it in place means getting buried the next time the ground shifts.

Clearing rubble feels like betrayal. Throwing away the papers feels like erasing the years you spent building. Letting go of a relationship feels like erasing the love that once was. Walking away from a career feels like denying the effort you put in. But this is a misunderstanding. Clearing doesn't dishonor what was lost; it honors it by refusing to pretend it is still alive.

Each time I threw something away, I felt a piece of myself go with it, but I also felt lighter. Ritual helped. I named what I was discarding, read it aloud, then shredded it, not for drama, but for dignity. The past deserves witness.

Others have told me the same thing. A friend who finally cleared her late husband's closet said it was the first day she could breathe. Another who went bankrupt finally sold the office furniture he'd kept for a decade and admitted he wasn't going back, he was going forward into something else.

Not everything in the rubble should be discarded. Some fragments are worth carrying. Skills, values, and relationships that survived become the raw materials for the next build. But arrogance, shortcuts, and toxic habits must be left behind.

One friend kept a ledger with three columns: skills still usable, relationships still trusting, and beliefs still true. Everything else went. In six months, he wasn't back where he had been; he was somewhere better.

History proves this principle. When Japan rebuilt after WWII, it kept discipline, ingenuity, and cultural pride. It discarded militarism and expansionism. The result was a nation reborn without its most destructive impulses.

Reinvention is editing. You keep, repurpose, and remove until only what is congruent with your future remains. And it always feels worse before it feels better. Each act of clearing feels like a death, but grief is the only honest way to let the past loosen its grip. Denial is easier in the moment, but it chains you to the ruins.

Once grief has done its work, clearing becomes easier. You start to notice how much energy you were wasting preserving what could not be restored. You breathe more freely. The house looks bigger, the air feels lighter, and even your own reflection seems less haunted.

Momentum is everything. Clear one shelf, then one room, then one conversation you've been avoiding. The emptiness stops being punishment and starts being oxygen. The barren ground begins to look like potential.

I've come to believe collapse exists partly to do this for us, the demolition we would never choose ourselves. Left alone, we cling forever. Collapse forces the issue. It tears down what was rotting, humiliates us enough to stop pretending, and leaves us standing in the only place where we can begin again: cleared ground.

Clearing is not cruelty. It is stewardship. It is life's way of handing you a broom and saying: make space for something living.

Chapter 5 Exercise: The Rubble Map

Take a blank sheet of paper and divide it into three columns:

Physical Rubble: objects or documents from your old life you are still holding.

Emotional Rubble: memories, grudges, or regrets you keep replaying.

Identity Rubble: labels that no longer fit, "successful executive," "perfect parent," "reliable provider."

Choose one from each column. Remove, burn, or donate the physical piece. Write down the emotional piece and tear it up. Speak the identity piece aloud and release it.

Do this regularly. Clearing rubble isn't one act. It's a practice, a rhythm. Each time you let go of one piece, the ground beneath you becomes more solid. Only when the rubble is gone can the future stand.

Chapter 6: Choosing What to Keep

Clearing the rubble strips life down to bare ground, but bare ground is only a pause, not a plan. If reinvention were nothing but demolition, every collapse would graduate into wisdom by default. It doesn't. What comes next is slower, quieter, and far more exacting: deciding what survives the fire. In the immediate aftermath, almost everything looks contaminated. You scan the fragments of your old life and flinch at each one, tempted to torch the lot and march into the wilderness with nothing but stubborn breath in your lungs. The fantasy is seductive: total erasure, a spotless self, a clean horizon with no shadows. It's also untrue. Nobody starts from zero. Even after the worst collapses, you carry something. The only question is whether you choose the load or let it choose you.

When my life went down, I wanted to salt the earth. Touching anything from before felt like pressing fingers into a live wire. Work, marriage, friendships, reputation; every contact sparked shame. I told myself survival required a total burn. Start from nothing, answer to no one, live unmarked. It sounded like freedom. In practice, it was an amputation. I wasn't reinventing; I was cutting off everything I might need for the road ahead. Severe enough, and you don't feel lighter. You just bleed.

Discernment is where reinvention begins, and discernment moves at a different speed than collapse. Clearing is violent, cathartic, and decisive. Choosing is patient, iterative, and suspicious of easy answers. You pick up a piece of your former life and turn it in your hands like evidence. Is there still life here? Will this help me build, or does it carry poison in its seams? There are no shortcuts for that kind of seeing. It takes time, and it takes honesty that doesn't flinch when a beloved fragment reveals itself as a blade.

I misjudged the essentials at first. I decided that trust itself was the flaw and built a perimeter with no doors. It took too long to notice that distrust was corroding me faster than betrayal ever had. Trust wasn't the enemy; careless allocation was—the same with ambition. My ambition had sprinted me into shortcuts and denial, but ambition wasn't the culprit. Ungoverned ambition was. Turning the right direction, it could fuel rebuilding instead of collapse. The fragment wasn't rotten. My use of it was.

History favors the patient salvager. Lisbon, after the 1755 earthquake, didn't scorch everything flat; it kept the street grid that worked and rebuilt around it. Postwar Japan did not discard discipline, craft, or cooperative pride; it cut militarism and kept the engine of making things well. Rebuilding that endures isn't a museum of the past or a bonfire of it. It's curation with teeth.

The trouble is that we're terrible curators under pressure. Collapse scrambles instinct. The same reflex that once saved you can sabotage you, and the same voice that pushed you off a cliff can sound like courage when you're desperate to move. I watched a man lose his reputation, sprint back into business on the same fuel of bravado and secrecy, and claim the echo as progress. He didn't rebuild; he repeated. Contrast that with a woman I met whose marriage ended overnight. She didn't declare intimacy a scam. She kept her capacity to love and revoked her tolerance for silence. In the next relationship, she insisted on ruthless honesty, including about her own fear. She salvaged the living fragment and left the lethal one behind. That choice did not erase pain; it converted it into structure.

Institutions learn this lesson, too, when they're forced to. Postwar Germany kept engineering brilliance, artistry, and education; it severed obedience without question and nationalism without brakes. The country that emerged

was not a rebirth from nothing. It was a recalibration from
what was still true.

My own recalibration started with humiliation disguised
as clarity. I had to admit some of my talents were genuine,
even though I had bent them toward ego and heat. I could
persuade. I could work. I could think strategically. Those
weren't the problem. The problem was the vector, not the
velocity. Keeping those meant binding them to different
aims and different guardrails. The opposite admission was
just as necessary. Some pieces had to go even though they
felt comfortable as skin: the obsession with appearance,
the reflexive chase for validation, the habit of tweaking
outcomes to land on my feet. Those weren't "quirks." They
were termites. Carry them forward, and the new frame
would sag like the old one, only faster.

This is not tidy work. You don't sit down one afternoon,
make two neat lists, and rise with a clean heart. Choosing
happens in the field, under the weather. You test a
fragment in real conditions, and sometimes it shows its
rot late. You discard something as useless and months
later realize it was a load-bearing beam you misread. You
keep something proudly and learn the hard way that it
was soaked in petrol. The process is iterative and a little
brutal. The only way through is a commitment to

unflinching accuracy, the kind that will not let nostalgia edit the inventory or shame incinerate everything indiscriminately.

I started to think of the work like panning a river. Most of what you hold will wash away, no matter how fondly you cradle it. That is not loss; it's clarity. You shake the pan, and the silt goes. What remains, even if small, can be enough to stake a claim. Collapse leaves a mountain of debris and a series of impulses: carry it all, burn it all, or sort. The first two feel dramatic. The last is the only one that builds a future.

I kept delaying the sort because I was exhausted by the sound of my own second-guessing. Eventually, I realized the fatigue came from dragging everything and choosing nothing. Collapse had already cost me enough. Why was I letting it keep charging interest by refusing to decide? So I began naming what was mine. At first, it felt like performance, like I was trying to convince myself of goodness. But over time, the kept fragments began to prove themselves in motion. Persistence showed up when I was alone and there was no audience to applaud. The love of words returned without the narcotic of praise and did not make me manic; it made me steady. A few friends stayed when the rest evaporated, and their loyalty turned out to be made of iron instead of smoke. Those weren't illusions. They were the parts that survived the burn because they were built to.

The hardest admission was permitting myself to keep anything at all. Shame wants total forfeiture. It insists that every strength is counterfeit, every talent disqualified, every future closed. But reinvention is not about what you deserve. It's about what you choose. The past does not issue refunds. You do not get back what was squandered. You do get to decide how to use what remains. That choice is the hinge.

Erasure will keep calling. There are days when the temptation to bury the past under concrete would be easier than living with it honestly. But erasure is just another mask. You cannot delete your former self. You can only decide how much of that person belongs in the next draft. I've watched people answer badly in both directions: some keep nothing and drift like empty boats, all performance and no keel; some keep everything and stage the same disaster on a new set. The few who truly rebuild are the ones who work with courage and patience. They honor what is alive, bury what is dead, and stop pretending not to know the difference.

Reinvention is not a miracle. It is a human standing in the debris of their own making, picking up pieces one by one, and saying yes or no with unblinking eyes. It is slow work. It is humbling work. It is the only work that gives the next chapter enough integrity to stand.

What stays, then? The pieces that are still true under pressure. The values that hold when nobody is watching. The skills that build something useful without demanding a lie to operate. The relationships that can tell the truth without using it as a weapon. What goes? The shortcuts dressed up as cleverness. The image management that turns you into a brand and leaves you hollow. The cravings that make every room a mirror. The alliances that only work if you pretend to be someone you can't bear.

If there is a single question that keeps the sort honest, it is this: Does this fragment demand pretending to keep it? Anything that requires constant self-deception to justify its place belongs to the fire. Anything that can be named accurately and used without lying about the past might belong in your hands again. Over and over, the test will be the same. Over and over, you will be tempted to soften the edge. Don't. The new structure inherits the integrity of its pieces.

By the time you choose a handful of fragments with conviction, the emptiness around you changes shape. It is no longer a void. It is a site. You cannot frame walls yet, but you can drive stakes and mark corners. You have enough to begin aligning your life around the parts that stayed true. The relief is subtle at first. A little more air in the room. A little less rehearsal of old arguments. A little courage that doesn't feel like caffeine. Then momentum arrives, not as adrenaline, but as rhythm.

The choosing never becomes glamorous. It does, however, become clean. Clarity is its own strength. And once you've carried only what's real for a while, the body remembers what it feels like not to lug a museum on your back. The past remains the past. It also becomes raw material. Both can be true.

Chapter 6 Exercise: The Salvage List

Make this a ritual, not a stunt. Sit at a table with a pen and a blank sheet. Draw a line down the middle. On the left, write Worth Keeping. On the right, write Must Release. Under Worth Keeping, list qualities, skills, values, and relationships that still feel alive when tested in real life. Not perfect. Alive. Under Must Release, list habits, illusions, cravings, and alliances that keep you rehearsing a role that collapsed. When the lists are quiet on the page, choose one from each side and run a seven-day field test. Put one kept fragment to work in a task that doesn't pay you in applause and see if it sustains you. Lay down one release fragment for a week, the validation chase, the image tweak, the old alliance, and observe who you are without it. At the bottom of the sheet, write in ink: I am not starting from nothing. I am starting from what is true. Read it every morning for seven days, not as a mantra, but as a contract.

The point is not to finalize an inventory you'll never revisit. The fact is to begin a habit of sorting that refuses to let nostalgia hoard or shame incinerate. Each time you choose, the ground under you firms. Each time you release, the next frame has one less hidden crack. This is the unseen labor of reinvention: not spectacle, not denial, but a steady salvaging of what survived and a burial for what didn't. From that, a life with clean lines can rise.

Chapter 7: The First Small Wins

After clearing the rubble and choosing what to carry, you expect the sky to split open and a soundtrack to kick in. It doesn't. Reinvention does not begin with a trumpet blast. It starts with something almost embarrassingly modest, the kind of act that would never make a highlight reel. That's the point. Small wins are quiet on purpose. They signal that life can move again without asking your nervous system to sprint on a broken ankle.

The hardest deficit after collapse is not talent or time; it is momentum. Shame turns simple motions into deadweight. You tell yourself it's laziness, but paralysis has a different texture. It sits you at the kitchen counter, eyes on a sink of dishes, arms heavy as if you're underwater. Collapse whispers that nothing you do matters, so why bother? Clearing the ground doesn't automatically silence that voice. It just makes the whisper audible. That's progress. Now you need proof.

My first proof was one page in a notebook. Not an outline, not a polished piece, just a page. The words were crooked. The lines doubled back on themselves. It did not change my circumstances. It did not restore my reputation. It did, however, break the seal between thought and action. My hand moved. A page existed that hadn't lived an hour before. I did one thing. That was enough for a day.

This is what people misunderstand about small wins. They imagine them as tokens, symbolic gestures you offer to keep your spirits up, like taping a slogan to a wall. They are not metaphorical. They are structural. A small win changes your state from "stopped" to "moving." That binary shift is everything. Neuroscience reduces it to chemicals; completion triggers dopamine, but the experience is simpler: a completed act tells your body the brakes aren't welded shut. Once, that's encouragement. Repeated, it's calibration.

I've watched this calibration rescue people who had no reason to trust themselves. A man who burned his life to the studs through addiction told me his first win was brushing his teeth before noon every day. On paper, that's nothing. In the physiology of collapse, it is a reassertion of agency. That one act created a spine for his morning, then for his afternoons, then for his week. A woman who lost her business began with one cooked meal a day. Not for aesthetics. For fuel. Her body steadied, and with it came the cognitive space to call creditors instead of hiding from them. Small wins are scaffolds, not confetti.

The problem is that we're trained to despise what isn't dramatic. We want to announce comebacks, not stack quiet repetitions. Collapse exploits that impatience. It says if you can't run, don't bother walking; if you can't rebuild everything, don't lift a finger. But the architecture of failure and the architecture of recovery are mirror images. Collapse arrives as a thousand tiny compromises that accumulate until the structure fails; rebuilding arrives as a thousand tiny completions that accumulate until a new frame holds.

The other trap is comparison. You will always find someone sprinting while you are learning to crawl. You will always be tempted to judge your one page against someone else's finished book. That is how you abandon a process that works in favor of a theater that doesn't. Your steps are not behind. They are yours.

Small wins rewire your story before they rebuild your life. The old story says you're stuck, finished, permanently defined by what burned down. One completed act is contradictory data. It does not erase the story, but it puts a crack in it. Light enters through cracks. Stack enough cracks and a narrative collapses under its own weight. That's not hope as a mood. That's hope as evidence.

I used to chase spectacle. New ventures. New declarations. New identities announced loudly enough to drown out doubt. Spectacle works until it doesn't, and it never works for long. When I tried to leap over the slow work of trust and rhythm, I landed in the same crater twice. The page, the dish, the walk, the call, these were the scale of acts that held. They were not impressive. They were reliable.

One of the first wins that mattered was answering a call I had been avoiding. It wasn't an apology yet, just the absence of another dodge. The conversation was slow and awkward. I hung up feeling exposed. But something had shifted. I had acted in the direction of the relationship instead of retreating. No one saw it. No one clapped. That anonymity made it real. Public gestures are easy to counterfeit. Private wins are hard to fake.

Small wins teach a different kind of confidence. Not the inflated confidence that struts because people are watching, but the grounded confidence that accumulates because you've kept more promises to yourself than you've broken in a row. At first, the streak is tiny and stupid: three days of doing the thing. Then a week. Then a month. The external situation may still be unstable, but the internal meter is no longer pinned to zero. You know you can act because you have acted repeatedly, without witnesses.

This is where humility becomes an asset instead of a bruise. Small wins force you to start where you actually are. Not where your pride insists you should be, not where your nostalgia claims you used to be, not where your critics say you'll never reach. Here. Now. One action. Humility shrinks the scope until it is doable, then does it. Pride inflates the scope until it is cinematic, then collapses under its own posture.

I met a man in a halfway house whose first win was waking up at the time he said he would. No job. No audience. No reward except alignment between intention and behavior. That alignment gave him something more durable than hype: predictability. From predictability came trust. From trust came responsibility. From responsibility came opportunity. The ladder wasn't magic. It was measurable.

Two enemies will show up as soon as you start: dismissal and escalation. Dismissal says your act is too small to matter. Escalation says your act must multiply every day or you're failing. Both are traps. The only metrics that matter in the beginning are repeatability and direction. Can you do this tomorrow without bargaining? Does it point your life in the right direction? If yes, it counts. If it counts, keep it.

There's a reason construction sites look unimpressive for a long time. Holes. Rebar. Mud. Nothing photogenic. Then, suddenly, a shape. The shape was inevitable the moment the footings cured, but you couldn't see it until the slow work stacked high enough to become visible at a glance. Small wins are footing work. They disappear into what they support.

Over time, the wins build identity as much as capacity. Each completion whispers over the old verdict: you are not what happened; you are what you are doing. That's not a slogan. It's a pattern. Patterns become character. Character becomes trajectory. The past doesn't vanish, but it stops monopolizing the plot.

Momentum is the gift that sneaks up on you. A page written today makes a page tomorrow less absurd. One honest conversation makes the next one less impossible. A bill paid reduces the static in your head just enough to make room for the second bill. Momentum doesn't feel like euphoria. It feels like the friction is decreasing. You still push, but the floor is less sticky, your steps less loud in your own skull.

Don't turn this into performance. The pressure to announce a comeback is just shame in a tuxedo. Reinvention is construction, not theater. The way you know you're building is that you could keep doing it if no one ever found out. In fact, assume no one will. If a habit only survives applause, it isn't a habit. It's a plea.

If there is one instruction I would hand to anyone standing on cleared ground, it is this: pick something so small it's hard to justify not doing it, and do it daily. Mock it in your head if you must. Just do it. Agency returns not as a roar, but as a rhythm. Rhythm is stronger than resolve. Resolve is a mood. Rhythm is a metronome.

You will be tempted, even after weeks of wins, to disrespect their scale. Resist the contempt. Collapse was built by small acts of neglect and denial. Reinvention will be built by small acts of attention and completion. The symmetry is not poetic; it's mechanical.

When I audit the season where my life began to move again, the public markers are easy to list: projects, partnerships, launches. None of them was the hinge. The hinge was a string of boring, private victories no one else would value if I handed them a list. They kept me from slipping back into the old loop. They freed enough bandwidth to see choices where before there had only been fog. They gave me back a self who could be trusted with larger levers.

If you need a test of whether you're on track, use this: Does your life contain a daily act so small it embarrasses your ego and strengthens your spine? If yes, you're building. If no, you're auditioning.

The first small wins do not announce a new chapter. They make it possible to write one.

Chapter 7 Exercise: Designing Your First Wins

Do not design a program. Design a proof.

Choose one act so small it borders on absurd. One page in a notebook. One call you answer instead of dodging. One walk around the block. One glass of water before coffee. Commit to seven consecutive days. Write it down in ink where you'll see it when you're tired and performative: I do this daily for one week.

At the end of each day, mark whether it happened. A check on a paper calendar is enough. The point is a visible trail of completions your brain can't argue with.

On day seven, write what changed. Not fantasies. Evidence. Did your mornings feel less sticky? Did a second act become easier because the first one existed? If the answer is yes, keep the act for another week and add a second of equal modesty. If the answer is no, choose a smaller act and try again. The problem is almost always scale, not will.

At the bottom of the page, write: Collapse was built in small acts. Reinvention will be too. Read it aloud, not because it's magic, but because your nervous system listens when your voice carries data.

Repeat until rhythm exists. Then protect the rhythm like oxygen. The size will take care of itself.

Chapter 8: Relearning Trust

Clearing the rubble and stacking your first small wins feels like progress, and it is. But there comes a moment when momentum alone is not enough. You've proven to yourself that you can act, but you have not yet risked being seen. Reinvention remains private until this point. Then comes the hardest part: trust.

Trust is not a single decision; it is a series of wagers. The first wager is that the world will not punish you for stepping out of hiding. The second is that if it does, you will survive anyway. Both are terrifying. Trust after collapse is like walking barefoot across ground you suspect might still be smoldering. You hesitate, test each step, and prepare to pull back at the first sign of heat.

My first act of trust was not dramatic. I picked up the phone and called a friend I had been avoiding for months. I had convinced myself he was angry, that he had written me off, that answering would mean hearing all the things I feared about myself spoken aloud. When he answered, I almost hung up. The conversation was slow, halting, and a little awkward. He did not deliver a lecture or a judgment. He asked how I was. I told the truth, not the whole story, not yet, but enough to break the silence. When I hung up, nothing had been fixed, but the call had done its work. I had stepped back into connection. That was the win.

Trusting after collapse feels unnatural because collapse teaches you that trust is dangerous. It warns you not to let anyone close, not to risk another blow. And it is not wrong to be cautious. Trust without discernment is not strength; it is exposure. But rebuilding requires more than private victories. At some point, you must risk handing a piece of your new life to another person and seeing whether it is held or dropped.

This is why self-trust must come first. Before I could trust anyone else, I had to trust myself not to sabotage my own progress. I had to believe that if I shared a truth, I wouldn't immediately backpedal or manipulate to protect my image. I had to think that I could survive someone else's disappointment without collapsing again. Self-trust is the foundation. Without it, every attempt at external trust is performance, a way to earn approval rather than a way to live honestly.

I began by trusting myself with small promises: I will write one page. I will keep this appointment. I will say what is true even if it feels risky. Every time I kept a promise, I added one brick to the wall of self-trust. When I broke a promise, I rebuilt instead of abandoning the wall entirely. Over time, I noticed that I no longer flinched before speaking the truth. I no longer second-guessed every instinct. Trust had begun to take root inside before I asked for it outside.

From there, I extended trust in layers. First, to a few people I believed could handle my fragile honesty, not necessarily my oldest friends, but the ones who had proven capable of sitting with discomfort without rushing to fix or judge. Then to slightly larger circles: colleagues, collaborators, neighbors. Each time, the risk grew. Each time, I learned who could be trusted and who could not. Some people did exactly what I feared. They judged, gossiped, or disappeared. Their reactions hurt, but they also clarified. Trust does not mean keeping everyone. It means finding who belongs in the next chapter.

Communities know this pattern well. After a disaster, the first step is clearing and stabilizing, but sooner or later, someone must open the doors again. Neighbors begin to gather, decisions are made collectively, and trust is rebuilt one meeting, one handshake, one shared meal at a time. Institutions do the same when they try to recover from failure; they don't demand instant faith, they offer transparency, small acts of accountability, and visible consistency. Trust accumulates slowly, but once enough layers form, it becomes self-sustaining.

The most surprising thing about trusting again is how much lighter life feels when it works. The first successful risk is a revelation: maybe the world is not as hostile as you feared. Maybe you are not as permanently marked as you believed. When someone receives your truth with grace, or even just neutrality, the shame that had been screaming in your head loses volume. You see that judgment exists, yes, but so does mercy. You see that rejection is survivable, but connection is irreplaceable.

None of this makes trust easy. Every act of trust is still a risk. Some will fail. Some will hurt. But each act teaches you something, even the ones that go badly. They teach you who cannot be trusted, where your boundaries need reinforcement, and where you must keep your guard up. Trust is not about being naïve. It is about refusing to let fear run your life.

I often think of the people I have watched rebuild trust slowly. One man I knew began by sharing a single secret with his sponsor in recovery. When it was met with acceptance instead of condemnation, he shared another. That process, repeated, taught him that vulnerability could coexist with respect. A woman I met after a divorce made herself go to dinner parties again, even though every cell in her body wanted to hide. The first few were miserable, but over time she found new friends, new laughter, and a new version of intimacy. Each of them built a new network of connections the same way you stack small wins: one deliberate step at a time.

Trust is not the final step of reinvention, but it is the first one that reintroduces you to the world. It turns reinvention from a solitary act into a relational one. It invites witnesses, and with witnesses comes accountability. You are no longer just rebuilding for yourself; you are rebuilding in public. That isn't very comforting, but it is also freeing. The new life you are building becomes visible. It becomes real.

Chapter 8 Exercise: The Trust Ladder

This practice is meant to help you rebuild trust gradually, layer by layer, until it becomes part of your rhythm again.

List three people you could risk trusting in a small way. Choose one that feels challenging but not dangerous.

Decide on a single act of trust. Share a small truth, ask for a minor favor, or let them see one part of your life you've been hiding.

Notice what happens next. Pay attention not just to their response but to how your body reacts, fear, relief, tension, calm. Write it down.

Repeat weekly, increasing the risk slightly each time. Move from low-stakes trust (casual conversations, minor truths) to higher-stakes trust (apologies, confessions, meaningful collaboration).

Review after a month. Which relationships deepened? Which ones proved unsafe? Which acts strengthened your self-trust regardless of outcome?

Trust grows through practice, not theory. Each rung on the ladder strengthens both your confidence in yourself and your ability to stand in the world without armor. The goal is not to make yourself invulnerable but to make yourself strong enough to risk connection again.

Part III: Reinvention as a Skill

Chapter 9: Reinvention Is Repetition

By the time you've cleared the rubble, chosen what to keep, and stacked your first small wins, something unexpected happens: reinvention stops feeling dramatic and starts feeling ordinary. The moment that once felt like a turning point gives way to something quieter, a rhythm. This is where most people lose the plot. They imagine reinvention as a single cinematic moment, the day they "got their life back." But reinvention isn't a single moment. It's repetition.

The work is not done when you have your first breakthrough. It begins there. Clearing rubble once doesn't mean it will stay clear forever. Choosing what to keep is not a one-time epiphany but an ongoing curation. Small wins must be repeated until they stop being "wins" and start being life. Repetition is what turns fragile progress into something unshakable. Without it, collapse waits patiently for you to slip. With it, you turn survival into identity.

This is where reinvention quietly claims its cost. When the novelty of change fades, when the applause (if there ever was any) dies down, when there are no more dramatic milestones to announce, that is when repetition matters most. I remember this season in my own life with brutal clarity. The first weeks of rebuilding had felt intoxicating, every act of consistency a small triumph. But by month three, it was just boring. Wake up at the same time. Write the page. Keep the promise. Again. Again. Again.

I craved drama. I wanted a leap to prove to myself that I had changed. I wanted something spectacular to show the world that collapse was behind me. So I reached for grand gestures, and, predictably, I stumbled. I nearly sabotaged everything I had built because I confused intensity with depth. The truth is, reinvention doesn't need spectacle. It needs rhythm.

Recovery programs understand this better than anyone. "One day at a time" is not a cliché. It is a recognition that change is not a single decision but the repetition of that decision so many times that it becomes instinct. Sobriety is not dramatic in its daily form. It is saying no again, every morning, every night, until the choice becomes a reflex.

History bears this out. Nelson Mandela did not become Nelson Mandela during his first year of imprisonment. He became Nelson Mandela over twenty-seven years of repeated discipline, reading, writing, negotiating, and waiting. Thomas Edison did not create the lightbulb with a single flash of brilliance. He repeated experiment after experiment, failure after failure, until failure itself became progress.

I learned this lesson most clearly when I kept my first promise to myself for the tenth time. It felt almost hollow. No one was watching, nothing visible had changed, but slowly, repetition softened the voice in my head that insisted I was unreliable. I didn't wake up one morning feeling trustworthy. I accumulated proof, one small act at a time, until the evidence outweighed the verdict shame had written against me.

Repetition feels unimpressive to outsiders. Nobody cheers for the fifteenth day in a row of doing what you said you'd do. Nobody claps because you kept writing after the first rush of inspiration faded. But applause was never the point. Reinvention is not theater; it is construction. And construction is boring until the frame is finally strong enough to stand on its own.

The paradox is that the boredom eventually becomes freedom. What begins as drudgery slowly becomes rhythm. The page gets written before you even think about it. The morning routine stops feeling like an act of heroism and becomes as ordinary as tying your shoes. This is the quiet miracle of repetition: it moves change out of the realm of willpower and into the realm of identity.

One morning, months after my collapse, I realized I had sat down to write without a battle in my head. I was writing before I knew I had begun. That was the moment I stopped trying to become a writer and realized I already was one. Repetition had carried me across the invisible threshold where effort becomes instinct.

This is the true payoff of repetition: not the act itself, but the person you become by doing it. Collapse had convinced me that I was unreliable, that my word, to myself or anyone else, was worthless. Repetition rewrote that story without speeches, without affirmations, simply by proving the opposite day after day.

Anyone can muscle through a season of intensity. Anyone can white-knuckle their way through a few months of change. But without repetition, collapse waits just outside the door. Repetition is what makes reinvention sustainable. It doesn't just build a life; it maintains it. It guards against erosion. It makes you someone who knows how to keep showing up when the novelty has worn off.

And here's the paradox worth embracing: the more boring your days look, the more likely you are to build something real. Collapse thrives on drama. Reinvention thrives on rhythm. The very thing you're tempted to resist, the monotony, is the thing that makes you unshakeable.

Chapter 9 Exercise: Building the Repetition Loop

Choose one act. Pick a single behavior tied to your reinvention, something small but meaningful, like writing a page, taking a daily walk, or telling one truth a day.

Commit for 30 days. The point is not scale but consistency. No make-ups, no doubling later.

Track it visibly. Mark each completion on a calendar, journal, or wall chart. The record matters; it's your visible proof.

Observe resistance. On the days you don't want to act, write down your excuses. Seeing them in ink drains their power.

Reflect weekly. Write a short note about how the practice feels: easier, harder, automatic, mechanical, so that you can see the shift over time.

Review after 30 days. Look at the pattern you've created. If the act is becoming automatic, keep it. If it still feels fragile, repeat the loop until the hesitation fades.

Repetition is not glamorous, but it is the hinge on which the whole reinvention turns. The new self is built the same way the old one was, act by act, day by day, until it is no longer what you are doing but who you are.

Chapter 10: Navigating Setbacks Without Collapsing Again

The first time a setback hit after my collapse, it nearly sent me back to the ground. It wasn't even catastrophic, just a deal falling through, a friend withdrawing, a reminder that the world still had teeth. But it felt like proof that everything I had rebuilt was a lie. This is the cruelest part of reinvention: the first real test. The moment where life asks, "Was all that work real, or was it just a phase?"

Setbacks are not just events; they are temptations. They whisper that nothing has changed, that collapse is waiting just offstage, that you might as well give up now and stop pretending you've moved on. If you let them, they will rewrite the entire story you've been building. The challenge is not avoiding setbacks; that's impossible. The challenge is refusing to let them trigger a collapse all over again.

I used to think the difference between those who stay standing and those who crumble again was strength. But it isn't. It's a strategy. Strength might get you through one bad day. Strategy gets you through ten. And reinvention, if it is to last, must be designed for endurance.

The first strategy is naming the setback for what it is: a setback, not a collapse. That distinction matters. Collapse is total, existential, identity-shattering. A setback is frustrating, discouraging, painful, but survivable. If you treat every setback as if it's the end, you will live in a cycle of endless false collapses, each one undoing you more completely. Naming it accurately keeps the wound from becoming mortal.

When I faced my first post-collapse failure, I panicked. My mind raced straight to catastrophe. I told myself I was a fraud, that everything I'd built was just a temporary disguise, that this one failure was proof I hadn't changed. That spiral nearly became self-fulfilling. But then I did something new: I stopped. I took inventory. Instead of asking, "What does this say about me?" I asked, "What does this actually change?" The answer, when I was honest, was surprisingly small. The deal was gone. My effort was wasted. But I was still standing. My integrity was still intact. My new habits were still holding. The setback hurt, but it didn't define me.

This is the crucial shift. After a collapse, you can't control how the world treats you, but you can control how you interpret the next punch. The skill is staying present enough to separate inconvenience from identity.

History is full of people who stumbled without falling. After Abraham Lincoln lost multiple elections, he didn't rewrite his entire story as a failure. After Nelson Mandela was humiliated and sidelined early in the ANC's struggle, he did not declare the fight over. Both treated setbacks as data, not as prophecy. That distinction saved them, and it will save you.

The second strategy is building shock absorbers into your life. This means refusing to live so close to the edge that one mistake destroys you. Before my collapse, I lived with no margin, financially, emotionally, or relationally. One crisis was enough to take me down. Now I build buffers. Not just money buffers, but time buffers, energy buffers, trust buffers. I no longer run every day at a sprint so that when I get hit, I have space to absorb the blow.

The third strategy is ritualizing recovery. Setbacks will always sting, and pretending otherwise only drives the pain underground. When something goes wrong now, I give it a container. I let myself be angry for one night. I write about it for one page. Then I decide on one action, not a dozen, just one, to take the next morning that moves me back toward the center. That ritual keeps the setback from metastasizing into despair.

This is where many people falter. They use setbacks as an excuse to torch the progress they've made. One broken promise becomes a reason to abandon the entire practice. One lost friendship becomes evidence that they are unlovable. One relapse becomes permission to sink all the way back into the old self. This is not just self-sabotage; it is surrender.

The antidote is remembering the long game. Reinvention is not about perfection. It is about persistence. The people who sustain reinvention are not the ones who never slip; they are the ones who refuse to turn a slip into a spiral. They get back up faster each time, until the getting up becomes instinct.

Setbacks are also teachers. They show you where your structure is still fragile. When a setback rattles me, I ask: What did this expose? What weakness did this reveal? Sometimes it's a blind spot I didn't know I had. Sometimes it's an overconfidence that crept in while I wasn't looking. Each lesson becomes another brick in the foundation.

Over time, setbacks lose some of their terror. Not because they stop hurting, but because you stop confusing pain with finality. You start to trust that pain is a signal, not a verdict. And when you can feel pain without unraveling, you become dangerous in the best sense: resilient, adaptable, unbreakable.

The final strategy is refusing to go back to hiding. Setbacks tempt you to disappear, to retreat into the old life where nobody can see you fail again. But reinvention dies in hiding. The only way through is forward, in public if necessary. Each time you reappear after a setback, you prove to yourself that collapse no longer has the power to erase you.

The truth is, you will face more setbacks. Reinvention does not buy immunity from loss, betrayal, or failure. It buys capacity. The next punch will land, but you will not shatter. The ground will shake, but you will know how to steady yourself. And that is the real reward of doing this work: not that life becomes smooth, but that you stop being so easily undone.

Chapter 10 Exercise: Setback Autopsy

Write down your latest setback. Be specific: what happened, who was involved, what was lost.

Name the emotions. Anger, grief, fear, write them without censoring.

Separate fact from story. Write two lists: "What Actually Happened" and "What I Told Myself It Meant." Notice the gap.

Identify one action. Choose a single step to take that keeps you moving forward. Make it small and specific.

Record the lesson. Ask: What weakness did this setback reveal, and how can I address it?

Do this each time a setback comes. Over time, you will build a record not just of failures, but of recoveries. And that record is how you prove to yourself that collapse is not inevitable.

Chapter 11: The Long Game of Reinvention

Reinvention is not a weekend project. It is not a single cathartic moment where you shed your old life like a snakeskin and emerge permanently transformed. That fantasy sells books and coaching programs, but it does not match reality. Reinvention is a long game. It unfolds in seasons, not in sudden bursts. The hard truth is that you will have to keep doing the work, again and again, long after the rubble is cleared, the first wins are stacked, and the people around you have stopped watching.

This is the part no one glamorizes. The crisis is dramatic, the clearing cathartic, the first steps inspiring. But the long game is quiet. It asks for repetition, routine, and resilience when nobody is cheering. The danger at this stage is subtle: you start to think you've "made it back." You relax the disciplines that carried you this far. You stop doing the daily habits, stop reflecting, stop guarding the edges of your life. And just like that, erosion begins again.

The truth is that collapse doesn't make you immune to future collapse; it just makes you more aware of how easily it can happen. The long game is about building guardrails that keep you from drifting back toward the same cliffs. It is about designing a life that makes it harder to repeat the patterns that once destroyed you.

For me, the long game meant establishing non-negotiables. Daily writing, weekly reflection, monthly financial reviews, quarterly conversations with people who told me the truth even when I didn't want to hear it. None of these habits is glamorous. Nobody claps when you keep a journal for the 217th day in a row. But that's the point. Reinvention must stop being performative and become maintenance.

This is also where boredom becomes a test. In the early stages, everything feels dramatic: the pain, the breakthroughs, the first fragile victories. Later, reinvention becomes mundane. You wake up and repeat the same choices day after day. You choose honesty again, discipline again, humility again. The temptation is to chase a new crisis, to create drama just to feel alive. I have done this, sabotaged my own stability because stability felt dull. The long game taught me that boredom is not a sign of failure. It is a sign that the structure is finally holding.

History reminds us that the nations and organizations that endure are not those that rebuild quickly but those that establish rhythms of renewal. Japan rebuilt after the

Second World War not with a single heroic decade but with decades of iteration, investment, and discipline. The same is true at the personal level. You cannot rush maturity. You cannot shortcut integration. What you can do is commit to staying on the path, even when the path is unremarkable.

This stage also requires accepting that not everyone will stay with you. Some people were drawn to the drama of your collapse and early recovery, but they have no interest in walking with you through the slow work of maintenance. Others preferred the old version of you and quietly withdrew because the new you doesn't serve their needs. This can sting, but it is part of the long game. The ones who remain are the ones who value your growth more than your performance.

There will be temptations to test your progress, to see if you can get away with old shortcuts now that you are "stronger." I fell into this trap more than once, taking on too much too quickly, ignoring the disciplines that kept me grounded, thinking I was immune. The long game is humbling because it reminds you that you are never immune. You will always be one or two bad decisions away from another collapse. That isn't fatalism, it's vigilance.

Vigilance does not mean living in fear. It means living awake. It means staying honest when lying would be easier, slowing down when rushing feels seductive, and asking for help before the crisis forces you to. It means paying attention to the early warning signs: the shortcuts creeping back in, the relationships fraying, the corners of your mind you'd rather not examine. The earlier you catch these, the less dramatic the course correction needs to be.

The long game also requires recalibration. The habits and systems that saved you in year one may become too rigid in year three. What was once a lifeline can become a prison if you refuse to adjust. I learned this when my writing practice became obsessive, a way to control rather than to create. I had to loosen my grip to allow the practice to evolve. Reinvention is not just about repetition; it is about iteration. You keep the rhythm, but you adjust the tempo as life changes.

This is why the long game is where the deepest growth happens. Collapse strips you bare, clearing the ground. The early wins prove you can move again. But the long game is where character is forged. It is where you stop being defined by collapse and start being defined by what you consistently choose afterward.

Looking back, I see that the most important work of my life was not clearing the rubble or even building the first structures. It was showing up, day after day, when there was no applause, no visible breakthrough, just the slow, steady proof that I was still here. That proof, accumulated over the years, became the foundation of trust, not just with others, but with myself.

This is the quiet gift of the long game: the day you realize that collapse is no longer the most interesting thing about you. That your story is no longer frozen at the worst moment. That you have lived enough days, chosen enough good choices, built enough new patterns that the collapse has been absorbed into something larger. Not erased, not forgotten, integrated.

Chapter 11 Exercise: Designing Your Long Game

List Your Non-Negotiables. Identify three practices that keep you grounded, daily, weekly, or monthly, and commit to protecting them.

Audit for Drift. Write down the last time you felt yourself slipping back toward old habits. What were the early warning signs? How will you catch them sooner next time?

Plan for Boredom. Decide now what you will do when the work of reinvention feels dull. Write down a healthy response, not sabotage, not crisis-seeking.

Schedule Re-Calibration. Once a quarter, review your systems. Are they still serving you, or have they become rigid? Adjust before they become a cage.

The long game of reinvention is not glamorous, but it is the most powerful stage. It turns survival into stability, stability into growth, and growth into wisdom. When you play the long game, collapse stops being the center of your identity and becomes just one chapter in a much larger story, a story you are still writing.

Chapter 12: Reinvention as Second Nature

There comes a point when you stop thinking of yourself as someone clawing out of collapse and start simply living differently. At first, reinvention is all strain, clearing rubble feels like manual labor, choosing fragments feels like surgery, small wins feel fragile, and repetition feels mechanical. The long game tests your patience. But if you keep going, something begins to shift. What once felt like defiance starts to feel like rhythm. The fight quiets. You no longer have to wrestle yourself into action every morning. You just act.

The first time I noticed this, it startled me. For months, every choice had been deliberate. Wake up on time. Write a page. Return the phone call you didn't want to return. No shortcuts. No cheating. Each choice had been a test of willpower. Then, one morning, I had written, answered calls, and cleared my inbox before noon, and only later did it hit me that I hadn't hesitated once. The old inner debate had gone silent. There had been no negotiation, no bargaining, no fear. I had just lived differently, as if it were the most natural thing in the world.

That was the first glimpse of reinvention settling into my bones. It wasn't a grand moment or a ceremonial line in the sand. It was quiet, almost unremarkable. But it was real. I was no longer trying to reinvent myself. I was simply living as the person I had been working so hard to become.

I've seen this same turning point in others. A friend who had fought alcoholism for decades told me about the night he realized he had crossed over. Someone offered him a drink, and he said no, without flinching, without tightening, without running a mental checklist. He didn't tell the story as a triumph; he barely mentioned it at all. But in that casualness was the evidence. Sobriety had stopped being a choice he made every moment. It had become who he was.

This is what second nature feels like: the scaffolding is still there, but you're no longer clinging to it. The daily disciplines are still happening, but they've faded into the background. You no longer spend energy proving you can do them. You simply do them. The work that once felt exhausting now frees up capacity, because you are no longer fighting yourself just to show up.

The more I lived inside second nature, the more I realized it wasn't just about survival anymore. Collapse had forced me into rebuilding, but second nature gave me something collapse could never take back: stability. Stability created space to think about the future differently. The question shifted from "Can I make it through today?" to "What kind of life will this build over the years?" That question is the beginning of vision.

Identity is not formed by inspiration; it is formed by repetition. When the repetitions are strong enough, you stop thinking about them. You stop noticing them. And that is the real sign that reinvention is taking hold, when you no longer have to spend energy remembering who you want to be. You simply are.

But second nature is not invulnerable. This is the stage where many people drift, forgetting that what feels automatic can still erode. I once knew a man who built a hard-won reputation for reliability. People trusted him, admired him. But he mistook second nature for permanence. He let small shortcuts slide. He skipped the disciplines that had rebuilt him. Within two years, the stability was gone. His collapse wasn't as dramatic this time, but it was just as painful, because he had tasted freedom and lost it.

That is the danger of second nature, complacency. It feels permanent, but it isn't. Permanence is an illusion.

Reinvention is a way of living, not a state you graduate into. Second nature must be tended like a garden. If you keep showing up, keep reinforcing the grooves you've worn; it deepens. If you neglect it, weeds return fast.

And yet, when it's cared for, second nature is the closest thing to freedom collapse will ever allow. You no longer wake up dreading the ruins. You no longer have to prove to yourself that you can stand. You simply stand. You simply live. The freedom is quiet, almost anticlimactic, no applause, no cinematic breakthrough. But it is durable. It is the kind of freedom that does not depend on adrenaline or external validation.

Second nature also ripples outward. People begin to notice your steadiness. They lean on it. They trust you with things they wouldn't have before. Your stability becomes part of their scaffolding. That weight can feel heavy, but it is also a sign that your reinvention has become visible. Your identity has stopped being just about you.

I have seen this happen in recovery communities: the person who was once shaking in the corner becomes the one others turn to for strength. Their sobriety, once precarious, becomes a beacon. They don't have to preach it; they just live it, and others borrow from it until they've built their own. This is when reinvention stops being personal and becomes cultural; it stabilizes not just you, but the people around you.

Cultures do this, too. Nations that survive collapse embed second nature into their institutions. Japan's pacifism, South Africa's reconciliation process, Germany's postwar constitution, these weren't single acts of will. They were deliberate attempts to make reinvention the default, to make it harder to go backward. They required reinforcement, vigilance, and decades of tending, but they turned fragile decisions into a national identity.

When reinvention becomes second nature, you stop asking whether you can keep going. You simply do. You live as if collapse is no longer in charge of the story. That doesn't mean you're safe forever. It means you've built enough strength to keep living without checking over your shoulder every five minutes.

Chapter 12 Exercise: Anchoring Second Nature

Name Your Defaults. Write down three behaviors or routines that now feel natural but once required effort. These are your second-nature wins.

Trace the Journey. For each, write down how hard it once was to do them. Remembering the cost keeps you from taking them for granted.

Design Reinforcements. Create a small ritual to keep each groove alive, a weekly review, a monthly reflection, a friend who asks you hard questions.

Spot the Cracks. Identify one area where your second nature still feels fragile. Write it down, and create a safeguard so it doesn't backslide.

Extend Outward. Name one way your stability already helps others and one way you can offer that support deliberately.

At the bottom of the page, write: Second nature is not final nature. It is a practice I live every day.

Part IV: The Long Game

Chapter 13: The Discipline of Continuity

A single comeback does not prove reinvention. It is proven by whether you can stay standing. Most people imagine reinvention as a dramatic moment: the comeback speech, the public announcement, the new venture that signals redemption. But those moments are peaks, not foundations. Real reinvention lives in the valleys, in continuity. The question is not whether you can rise once, but whether you can keep growing, day after day, year after year, without sliding back into collapse. Continuity is the discipline that makes reinvention endure.

From the outside, continuity looks almost boring. There are no fireworks in keeping your word quietly for ten years. No headlines celebrate the person who just keeps showing up. But this is where the real work lives. Continuity is what turns recovery into identity. Without it, reinvention stays fragile, a phase you could exit at any moment.

I learned this the hard way. The first year after my collapse, I was fierce about my routines. I never missed a commitment. The fear of falling back kept me sharp. But in the second year, that fear softened. The rubble was mostly gone. Life felt steady again. That's when I began to drift, skipping a routine here, taking a shortcut there, cutting corners that had once been non-negotiable. At first, nothing fell apart. That was the most dangerous part. The lack of immediate consequence convinced me I was safe. But slowly, the structure I had built began to loosen, and I realized how close collapse always remains. Reinvention doesn't end when the crisis ends. It must be carried forward deliberately, or erosion begins.

Continuity demands vigilance, not paranoia, not rigidity, but clear-eyed attention. It asks you to practice the same disciplines when you're tired, when you're bored, when there's no applause to motivate you. It means refusing to believe you've "graduated" from the work that saved you. The ego wants a finish line. Continuity denies it. It says: This is your life now.

At first, continuity can feel like a leash. You resent the rules you set for yourself, the rituals that tie you to the path. But over time, the leash becomes rhythm. The routines that once felt like obligations become anchors. Continuity stops being about willpower and starts being about trust, trust that the structure you've built will hold even on the days you feel weak.

I've watched this play out in people decades past their collapse. The ones who last aren't the ones chasing dramatic reinvention every few years. They're the ones who quietly keep the same commitments, season after season, until steadiness becomes their reputation. Continuity is their rebellion against collapse.

This does not mean rigidity. Continuity isn't about freezing yourself in place. It's about never abandoning the project. The scaffolding may evolve, the habits may change form, but the essence is persistence. Collapse thrives on neglect. Reinvention thrives on sustained motion.

History makes the same case. Civilizations that endure are not those that refuse to change, but those that adapt without losing their thread. Japan rebuilt through kaizen, small improvements compounded over decades. Britain's monarchy redefined its powers but kept its symbolic presence alive. Continuity is not repetition for its own sake; it is the ongoing refusal to let neglect undo what was hard-won.

For me, continuity became real when adrenaline and guilt stopped working. In the early months, adrenaline kept me moving, the urgency of proving to myself I wasn't finished yet. Guilt kept me from slacking because every mistake still echoed with shame. But both burned out. What replaced them was structure: rules that didn't depend on mood, routines that didn't require negotiation, guardrails that carried me even on bad days.

That's the secret of continuity: it's not about strength in the moment. It's about designing a life that does not require strength every moment. You cannot white-knuckle reinvention forever. If every day requires maximum willpower, you will eventually fail. Continuity builds a system that makes good choices easier and bad decisions harder.

This is why recovery programs are built on ritual. Meetings, sponsors, and daily inventories, none of them rely on inspiration. Athletes do the same. They train on schedule, not when they feel like it. Spiritual traditions understand this too: monks pray at set hours, whether or not they think holy. The rhythm creates the strength. Continuity is not the absence of struggle; it is the infrastructure that carries you through the battle without collapsing.

The discipline of continuity is also a discipline of perspective. If you measure success only by dramatic milestones, you will get discouraged. Continuity teaches you to measure success by motion. A musician isn't great because of one concert; they are great because they practiced every day when no one was watching. Reinvention works the same way. You prove nothing in a week. You prove everything in a decade.

Chapter 13 Exercise: Continuity Anchors

Identify Your Non-Negotiables. Write down three practices that keep collapse at bay, the minimum habits that, if dropped, signal you are drifting.

Tie Them to Rhythms. Attach each to a time, place, or ritual. Make them automatic—morning pages, Sunday reviews, first-coffee reflections.

Create Failsafes. Write one safeguard for each anchor: a friend who will call you if you miss, a calendar reminder that won't go away until you act.

Track Quietly. Mark completion each week. No fanfare, no announcements, just a record that reminds you the line is holding.

Review Quarterly. Ask yourself: Are these anchors still strong? Do they need reinforcement or evolution? Adjust before they fray.

Continuity will never be glamorous, but it is the most radical act of reinvention. It refuses drama, refuses shortcuts, refuses to let collapse write the final word. It is the choice to stay in motion, year after year, until the life you have built is no longer at risk of falling apart but strong enough to hold you, no matter what comes next.

Chapter 14: Teaching Others Without Preaching

The moment you begin to live differently, people notice. You may not want them to, but they do. Collapse is public even when you think it's private. People saw the shortcuts pile up, the trust fray, the promises break. Even if they never said anything, they kept the memory. And when you begin to rebuild, they notice that too. Reinvention, once it takes root, is visible. The question is not whether others will see it; the question is what you will do with their attention.

The first temptation is to explain yourself. To declare your new identity. To package your wisdom. To make sure people know you've changed. I fell straight into that trap. After a few months of steady habits, I started turning conversations into lessons. I dropped advice where nobody had asked for it, as if I could talk people into seeing me differently. I told myself I was helping them avoid the mistakes I had made, but really, I was trying to speed up their verdict on me. And it backfired. People pulled away. They didn't need a lecturer; they needed proof.

That is the paradox of teaching reinvention: the less you try to teach, the more others learn. Preaching is loud. Embodied change is quiet. And quiet endures. People believe actions long before they think of explanations. When they see you living differently, steadily, without fanfare, that teaches more than any speech could. Your life becomes the evidence. Your continuity becomes the curriculum.

This isn't a call to silence. There are moments to speak, and when they come, words will have weight precisely because a visible record of change backs them. Without that, words sound hollow. With it, words simply confirm what others already see. Recovery communities know this truth well. They have a phrase: *attraction, not promotion.* You don't push your reinvention on anyone. You live it, and let the results speak. Those who are ready will notice. Those who aren't won't, and that is not your failure.

I've seen the same truth in apprenticeship systems. Masters rarely lectured about skill. They worked, and the apprentice watched. Lessons were not sermons; they were rhythms. Reinvention works the same way. The people around you will learn most from what you do, not from what you say.

The psychology behind this is simple: people resist being preached at because it feels like control. No one likes to be told what to do, especially by someone they remember collapsing. Advice can sound like hypocrisy, even when it's sincere. But presence doesn't trigger that resistance. Watching someone live differently stirs curiosity instead of defensiveness. And curiosity is the doorway to change.

That's when questions start to come, quietly, hesitantly. "You don't get as angry as you used to. What changed?" "You seem calmer. What's different?" These aren't invitations for a sermon. They're invitations for a story. And that's what teaching without preaching really is: not instruction, but witness. Witnessing is different from prescribing. It doesn't tell someone what they must do; it offers them a living example and lets them decide what to take from it.

This is why three tools matter here: presence, humility, and storytelling.

Presence is not charisma; it's consistency. People learn from you when they stop bracing for volatility, when they know what version of you will walk through the door. In my collapse, my presence was erratic; people never knew if they'd get charm, anger, or withdrawal. Reinvention meant becoming someone steady enough that people no longer waited for me to break character. At first, every interaction felt like a test. Over time, continuity took over. The steadiness was no longer an act; it was me.

Humility is the antidote to the ego's urge to perform. Collapse strips you down, but survival can puff you up again if you're not careful. The moment you start acting like a prophet, you lose people. Humility keeps the story human and believable. When someone asks what changed, you tell it plainly, not as a sermon, not as a pitch, but as a witness. Humility invites curiosity instead of defensiveness.

Storytelling is the bridge. A lecture sounds like authority. A story sounds like an experience. Collapse left me with stories whether I wanted them or not: stories of failure, of clearing rubble, of starting over from scratch. When people asked, I gave them those stories, not as instructions, but as offerings. Stories let people place themselves inside the lesson. They see the choices, the costs, and the outcomes, and decide what to carry forward.

Patience is the fourth, silent tool. You don't get to decide when others will learn from you. Some will watch for years before they believe your change is real. Some may never believe at all. That isn't your problem. Your job is to keep living consistently. Over time, your reinvention lengthens its shadow. People may one day come to you and say, "Watching you gave me courage," and you'll be startled because you didn't even know they were paying attention.

History shows us this pattern. Gandhi's strength wasn't in fiery speeches but in visible, embodied consistency. His life was the argument. The women who sustained civil rights movements taught without preaching, cooking meals, hosting meetings, and singing through fear. Their presence taught more than a thousand manifestos could. They didn't convert people with rhetoric; they converted them with steadfastness.

I think of a man I knew who rebuilt quietly after prison. For years, he said nothing about redemption. He didn't declare himself changed. He just kept showing up, day after day. A decade later, he had a circle of people who trusted him deeply, some who didn't even know his past. His reinvention had taught them something profound: that collapse does not have to be final. And he never had to say it aloud.

This is the discipline of restraint: resisting the urge to prove yourself, resisting the ego's demand to be recognized, resisting the temptation to perform. The quieter you are, the stronger your life speaks. And when you do speak, the words will matter because they are backed by proof.

Chapter 14 Exercise: Quiet Proof

Choose One Habit to Make Visible. Pick a part of your reinvention that others can actually see, showing up on time, keeping your word, finishing what you start.

Keep It Consistent for 30 Days. No explanations, no announcements. Just quite proof.

Notice Who Notices. Write down who comments, who shifts their tone, who begins to trust again.

Resist the Lecture. When asked, answer simply, honestly, but don't perform.

Repeat. Add a second habit. Build a portfolio of undeniable proof until words become optional.

This chapter isn't about hiding. It's about living so steadily that your life does the talking. People will learn from you whether you want them to or not. The only question is whether what they know will be worth repeating.

Chapter 15: Collapse as Companion

Most people want the collapse to vanish. They want the rubble swept away, the scars hidden, the shame erased. They want reinvention to be a clean slate, as if the collapse never happened. I liked that too. But collapse never left. It didn't disappear when I rebuilt my routines. It didn't fade when I regained trust or even when success returned. Collapse stayed close. Sometimes it whispered, sometimes it lurked silently, but it was always there.

At first, I thought its presence meant I hadn't really changed. Surely, if I were fully healed, collapse would stop haunting me. But over time, I learned the opposite was true: reinvention is not about erasing collapse. It is about learning to carry it without letting it break you again.

Collapse becomes a companion. Not a friend, not exactly an enemy, but a presence you carry. It shadows your steps as a reminder of fragility. It keeps humility alive. It teaches vigilance, not paranoia, but wisdom. If you pretend collapse is gone, you set yourself up to repeat it. If you accept collapse as a companion, you learn to live with your scars instead of fighting them.

I first recognized collapse as a companion years after my most visible ruin. Life was steady, routines were strong, and relationships repaired. From the outside, it looked like the past had been buried. Then one night, after a minor failure, a promise broken, a small but meaningful slip, the old rush of shame hit like a flash flood. My chest burned, my stomach twisted, and the voice came: *See? Nothing has changed.* For a moment, I thought I was back in the rubble.

But then I noticed something new: I didn't spiral. I didn't run. I sat with it. I realized this wasn't a relapse. It was a collapse reminding me it still existed, waiting to see what I'd do. That recognition steadied me. The voice wasn't proof that I hadn't changed; it was proof that collapse would always remain close. My job was not to exile it but to live alongside it.

Self-help culture sells the fantasy of permanent transformation: you collapse once, you reinvent once, and then you live happily ever after. But collapse doesn't disappear. It lingers like scar tissue. And strangely, that is not a curse. It is a gift. Collapse as a companion keeps you honest. It denies you the illusion of invulnerability. The people most likely to collapse again are the ones convinced they're past it.

History proves this. After the Black Death, Europe built rituals of remembrance into its civic and religious life.

Tomb carvings, festivals, and architecture reminded people of mortality. Those who remembered adjusted their practices, improving sanitation, reforming trade, and developing medicine. Those who pretended the danger was gone were devastated when the next plague came. Collapse as a companion was not morbid; it was survival.

I once met a man who carried a fragment of his own collapse everywhere: a piece of the eviction notice from the day he lost his home. He kept it in his wallet, and every time he saw it, he remembered how arrogance and neglect had wrecked him. That scrap of paper didn't paralyze him. It steadied him. It was a guardrail that kept him from drifting too far.

Another woman told me that her divorce, which she once believed would kill her, sits beside her even in her happy second marriage. It's there in every argument, every choice to listen instead of dismiss, every moment she defends a boundary. Collapse is still present, whispering reminders of what neglect once cost her. Far from weakening her new marriage, it helps keep it alive.

Collapse as a companion is not romantic. It isn't noble, and it isn't a badge of honor. It broke you, and it could hurt you again if you grow careless. But when you accept its presence, you stop wasting energy trying to erase it. You stop needing the illusion of closure. Collapse becomes a sentinel, not a saboteur.

Recovery communities understand this instinctively. People there don't say "I was an addict." They say, "I am." Not because they expect relapse every day, but because they know collapse remains close. That humility protects them. The moment someone declares themselves "cured," collapse sneaks back through the cracks. Vigilance is not fear; it is maintenance.

When collapse becomes a companion, you stop living in illusions about your own invulnerability. You stop pretending you are beyond failure. That realism is oddly freeing. You are no longer afraid of the shadow because you know it. You've walked with it. You have survived alongside it. Collapse never leaves, but neither does it have to keep you captive. Its voice becomes less a threat and more a reminder: *pay attention, keep your guardrails strong, keep moving forward.*

That is the strange gift of collapse. Once it sits beside you, you are never free of it, but you are also never fooled again. You know what arrogance costs. You know what negligence destroys. And you know what it takes to rebuild. Collapse as a companion is uncomfortable company, but it is a company that saves you.

Chapter 15 Exercise: Naming Your Companion

Name Your Collapse. Write down the collapse that shaped you most. Be specific. Name it clearly so it cannot hide.

Describe Its Presence. How does it show up in your life today, a whisper, a jolt, a scar? Write what it feels like.

Turn It Into a Guardrail. Choose one way this memory can keep you steady, a ritual, a phrase, an object, and use it to remind you of what's at stake.

Review Monthly. Ask: Is collapse helping me stay grounded, or is it steering me? Adjust your response so it remains a companion, not a driver.

Chapter 16: Reinvention Without End

Reinvention does not finish. That is the secret most people do not want to hear. They want a final act, a closing scene, a point where they can say, "It's over, I made it back." I liked that too. I wanted to hang a framed certificate on the wall that said *redeemed.* But reinvention refuses to be a single event. It keeps unfolding. It keeps asking more of you. It keeps revealing new work to do.

At first, this felt exhausting. Wasn't the point to be done? Hadn't I cleared the rubble, sorted the fragments, stacked the wins, held the line through repetition? How much more was there to do? It took me years to see that this question came from the same impulse that had fueled my collapse: the craving for a finish line. Reinvention without end is not punishment; it is freedom. Because as long as there is no finish line, there is no failure for not having crossed it. There is only the next choice, the next day, the next step.

This is the shift: you stop treating reinvention as recovery and start treating it as a way of life. You stop thinking in terms of "back to normal" and start thinking in terms of forward motion. Collapse may have forced you to rebuild, but once you are standing again, you keep building, not because you must, but because you can.

I have seen this shift in others. A man I knew rebuilt his finances after bankruptcy, slowly, painfully, over nearly a decade. When he finally reached stability, he could have coasted. But he didn't. He kept learning, kept refining his systems, kept building not just wealth but wisdom. His life became about stewardship, not just survival. Reinvention became his permanent operating system.

This is what reinvention without end feels like: you no longer measure yourself against the moment of collapse. You measure yourself against what is possible now. You stop asking, "Have I made it back?" and start asking, "What am I making next?" That shift turns reinvention from a season into a stance, a way of holding yourself in the world.

Cultures that survive catastrophe know this truth. After the Great Fire of London, the city did not simply rebuild what was lost. It redesigned its streets, improved its water systems, and created fire codes. It kept reinventing long after the ashes cooled. That's why London did not burn in the same way again. Reinvention without end prevents the same disaster from becoming inevitable.

At this stage, the danger is complacency disguised as relief. You tell yourself you've learned the lesson, that collapse is behind you, that you can relax now. But collapse is never entirely behind you, as Chapter 15 reminds you, it travels with you as a companion. Reinvention without end is the decision to keep learning from it instead of resenting its presence.

I had to make peace with the fact that there would never be a "perfect" version of me. There would only ever be the version who chose, each day, to build a little more. Some days the work was structural, adding a new habit, repairing a broken trust. Some days it was subtle, choosing patience over control, forgiveness over pride. The point wasn't perfection. The point was movement.

This is why reinvention feels lighter over time, not heavier. In the beginning, every choice feels loaded with shame, as if one wrong step will collapse the whole fragile structure. But when you live long enough inside reinvention, you stop walking on eggshells. You walk with grounded feet. You know you can rebuild again if you have to. That confidence does not make you careless; it makes you bold.

Reinvention without end is not a life sentence. It is a declaration that you will not stop growing just because the crisis has passed. It is the refusal to let the collapse be the most interesting thing about you. It is the decision to keep becoming, not just to recover who you were but to outgrow even that.

Chapter 16 Exercise: The Open Horizon

Write Your "Finish Line" Fantasy. Be honest, what would you like to declare "done"? The relationship? The debt? The inner voice? Write it all down.

Cross It Out. Literally draw a line through the page. This is not to deny your progress but to remind yourself that there is no final arrival.

Name One Next Step. Instead of a finish line, choose a next horizon. What can you grow, deepen, or risk now that you could not when you were buried in rubble?

Create a Practice of Renewal. Once a year, set aside a day to review your life as if you were beginning again. What needs to be cleared? What fragments need to be re-evaluated? What wins need to be stacked?

Reinvention without end is not exhausting when you stop fighting it. It becomes the most honest way to live. Collapse stops being a single event and becomes the raw material for a lifetime of becoming. There is no arrival. There is only the next chapter, and the next, and the next, until the day you are gone.

Part V: Reinvention in Context

Chapter 17: Reinvention in Work

Work is one of the most ruthless mirrors of who you are. It doesn't care about your excuses or your past. It measures you every day, not by your intentions, but by your output, your presence, and your follow-through. That's why collapse feels so devastating when it touches your work. When you lose a job, a business, or a career, it's not just a financial wound; it's an identity wound. It tears away the story you've told yourself about who you are.

I know because I spent months after my collapse trying to outrun the professional humiliation. I polished résumés, pitched projects, networked harder than ever, all to prove I was still the person I used to be. The problem wasn't my skill set; it was my motive. Every move I made was about clawing back status, not about building something true. I wasn't working; I was performing.

That's the first trap of reinvention in work: confusing the hunger for redemption with the desire to create value. You don't need a job or a title to restore your worth. You need work that is honest enough to keep you grounded and demanding enough to force you to keep growing.

I have seen people face this test in a hundred different ways. A man I knew had run a company for two decades until it folded. When he started over, he took a junior job in a small firm, not because it matched his résumé, but because it gave him rhythm again. Showing up every morning, doing tangible work, earning trust slowly, that was his rehabilitation. Another friend turned her collapse into an apprenticeship. After years as a manager, she went back to entry-level work, learning from people she would once have supervised. She told me later that those months redefined her idea of leadership.

Reinvention in work is humbling. It asks you to trade prestige for traction, pride for learning. It forces you to confront the difference between doing what looks good and doing what actually builds something. Work becomes the proving ground where your rebuilt character is stress-tested.

The danger is rushing back too fast. I did this more than once, took on projects too big, too public, too soon. And when I inevitably stumbled, the shame hit twice as hard. Collapse taught me that work can't be used as a shortcut to redemption. You don't rebuild your reputation by announcing that you've changed. You rebuild it by showing up consistently until the evidence outweighs the memory of your failure.

History makes the same point. After the Great Depression, millions of people found dignity again, not through handouts but through the WPA and CCC programs that put them back to work. They built roads, parks, and schools. The work didn't just restore their income; it restored their confidence. The labor itself was part of the healing.

Work after collapse is not just about paying the bills. It is about practicing who you are becoming. Every email you send, every meeting you attend, every promise you keep becomes part of your reinvention portfolio. Over time, these small proofs accumulate. The world may not applaud them, but it notices.

This is why reinvention in work must start with honesty. What kind of work keeps you honest? What kind of work forces you to stay awake? What type of work allows you to create value without slipping back into the illusions that once destroyed you? These questions are uncomfortable, but they are the right ones.

The shift happens when you stop asking, "How do I get my old job back?" and start asking, "What is worth building now?" When you stop performing and begin contributing. When you stop measuring yourself by the corner office or the title and start measuring yourself by whether you are creating something that lasts.

Reinvention in work is not a single decision. It is a series of small ones, repeated until they become second nature: keep your word, tell the truth, do what you said you'd do even when no one is watching. These are not glamorous habits, but they are the ones that make a career, a business, a body of work that can stand.

Chapter 17 Exercise: The Work Reset

Inventory Your Work Story. Write down how your old career defined you, the roles, the titles, the identity you carried. Name what collapsed and why.

Separate Identity from Role. Underline what was real (skills, strengths, values) and cross out what was illusion (status, appearances, ego).

Choose Work That Rebuilds You. Identify one role or project that forces you to practice honesty, discipline, and value-creation. It does not have to impress anyone; it just has to keep you moving forward.

Commit to One Season. Give yourself three to six months of showing up to this work, even when it feels beneath you, even when it bruises your pride.

Review the Evidence. At the end of the season, write down what has shifted in your skills, your confidence, and your relationships. Let the proof tell you what to build next.

Reinvention in work is not about getting back to where you were. It is about becoming someone whose work no longer needs to be a disguise. It is about creating value so real that even if collapse comes again, and it might, you will not be shattered, because your worth will no longer be housed in a title.

Chapter 18: Reinvention in Relationships

When your life collapses, relationships become one of the most painful fault lines. Some fractures immediately. Some linger like ghosts. Some survive but are never quite the same. Collapse doesn't just take your job, your reputation, or your money; it redraws the entire map of who is willing to walk beside you.

At first, I wanted to keep everyone: friends, colleagues, acquaintances, anyone who had ever been part of my old life. I reached for them out of panic, terrified that losing them would make the collapse final. But here's the truth: collapse is a filter. It reveals who can hold you when you're stripped down and who was only there for the performance version of you.

The grief in this is almost unbearable. You watch people back away, not always maliciously, sometimes just out of discomfort, and it feels like betrayal. Sometimes it is betrayal. Sometimes it's just self-preservation on their part. But in those first months, it all feels the same: abandonment layered on top of failure.

The temptation is to chase them. To explain, to defend, to convince them you're still worth standing beside. I did this until it broke me. Collapse taught me that you can't strong-arm loyalty. People reveal who they are when you have nothing left to offer them but your presence.

I remember calling someone I considered a close friend after my public disgrace. They answered once, awkwardly, and then never picked up again. Each ignored call felt like another verdict. For months, I replayed that silence, trying to decide whether they were wrong for abandoning me or whether I was wrong for needing them. Eventually, I saw that neither was the point. The point was that the friendship belonged to the old life, and it could not survive in this one.

Reinvention in relationships means accepting that not every connection can be carried forward. Some must be let go, not in anger but in acknowledgment. They were good for a season, but that season has ended.

But letting go is only half of the work. The other half is deliberately choosing which relationships will be part of the new life you are building. This is where reinvention becomes dangerous if you are not careful. Collapse leaves you lonely, and loneliness makes you vulnerable. You will be tempted to fill the vacuum with anyone who will offer you validation, even if they are toxic, even if they reinforce the very patterns that destroyed you the first time.

I've seen this destroy people. A man I knew left a marriage that had collapsed under the weight of his lies, only to start dating someone who applauded the same behavior that ruined him. He rebuilt his life around the same patterns, and within a year, he was back in ruin. Collapse doesn't save you from your choices. You still have to choose differently.

The hard part is that trust feels impossible in the aftermath. After you've been judged, after you've been abandoned, after you've been betrayed, trusting anyone feels like handing them a weapon. The reflex is to harden, to protect yourself by refusing intimacy altogether. I did this for a long time, keeping everyone at a distance, convinced that safety lived in isolation. But isolation is its own kind of collapse.

Trust has to be relearned. Slowly, awkwardly, one small step at a time. The first time I told someone the unvarnished truth about my past, my voice shook. I waited for the judgment to land, for them to walk away. They didn't. They stayed. That one conversation became a blueprint for how to rebuild connection: not with everyone, not recklessly, but with those who had earned the right to know me as I really was.

Reinvention in relationships is not about surrounding yourself with cheerleaders. It is about curating a circle that is honest enough to tell you when you are slipping back into old patterns and kind enough to walk with you through the mess.

This curation process is brutal. It means acknowledging that some family members will never understand that some friends will always see you as your worst moment, and that some colleagues will never trust you again. It also means recognizing the quiet loyalty of those who stayed, not taking them for granted, and inviting new voices who are aligned with the life you are now trying to build.

History gives us examples of this kind of relational reinvention. After apartheid fell, South Africa faced a choice: vengeance or reconciliation. The Truth and Reconciliation Commission was imperfect, but it created space for honesty, confession, and forward motion. Personal reinvention requires the same: a process of truth-telling, grieving, and choosing who belongs in the next chapter.

Relationships are both the hardest and the most transformative part of rebuilding. Work can be rebuilt in solitude. Reputation can be repaired through action. But relationships require mutuality; they need someone else to meet you halfway. That is why they feel so risky and why they matter so much.

I learned that the goal is not to get back every relationship you lost. The goal is to build a network strong enough to hold the weight of the person you are becoming. That means fewer, deeper, truer connections. It means choosing substance over social performance. Invest in people who tell you hard truths, and don't waste energy on those who hold you back.

Chapter 18 Exercise: The Relational Ledger

Draw a Ledger. On one side, list the people whose presence strengthens you, challenges you, or gives you space to grow. On the other hand, list those whose presence keeps you tethered to the collapse.

Identify Patterns. Which of the second-column names are tied to old habits, old illusions, or toxic validation? Which first-column names are the ones that stayed when it was costly?

Take One Step. Call, text, or meet with one person from the first column and thank them for standing by you. Then take one small step to create distance from someone in the second. Not dramatic, just one step.

Repeat Monthly. This is not a one-time purge but an ongoing practice. Each month, ask: who belongs in this chapter, and who belongs in memory?

Reinvention in relationships is slow work, but it is the work that ensures you are not rebuilding in isolation. You are building a life supported by people who can hold you accountable, remind you who you are when you forget, and celebrate your progress without resenting it. This is not about having more friends. It is about building a circle that is as intentional as the life you are creating.

Chapter 19: Reinvention in Community

Reinvention is never purely personal. It might start in solitude, with your own rubble and your own reckoning, but sooner or later it runs headfirst into the world outside your door. A rebuilt life has to live somewhere. And that somewhere is a community, whether that means a town, a church, a team, a movement, or a circle of people who care enough to keep you tethered.

In the early days after the collapse, I avoided the community altogether. It felt like stepping into a room where everyone was whispering. I imagined every glance loaded with judgment. It seemed safer to stay away. But isolation turned out to be its own kind of ruin. Reinvention cannot remain an entirely private project because it needs friction to take shape. A life rebuilt in total solitude becomes fragile, untested. You need the pushback, the mirrors, the accountability that other people bring.

The first step in re-entering the community is terrifying because it feels like offering the world another chance to reject you. I remember the first time I walked back into a volunteer meeting months after my collapse. My pulse thudded in my ears. I waited for someone to confront me, to ask why I had shown my face. No one did. People were polite, even welcoming, but the real battle was inside me. I had to fight the instinct to flee before the meeting even started.

Community after collapse isn't about reclaiming your old place; it's about finding a new one. Some spaces will never take you back. Some people will never stop seeing you as the person you were at your worst. That's not cruelty; that's human memory. Reinvention in community means respecting that reality without letting it dictate your entire social existence.

Communities themselves can be unforgiving. They hold memory like sediment, slow to shift, slow to forget. In some cases, they cling to your past more tightly than you do. But communities can also be astonishingly redemptive. When South Africa faced the end of apartheid, it could have chosen vengeance. Instead, it convened the Truth and Reconciliation Commission. Imperfect, yes, but it created a space where confessions could be heard and forgiveness could be offered. That is what healthy communities do: they give people a way back.

Not every community is healthy. Some thrive on scapegoats. Some need your downfall to confirm their righteousness. Part of reinvention is learning which communities deserve your presence and which only want to keep you in exile. This is not bitterness; it is discernment. A community that feeds on shame will keep you small. A community that challenges you but also wants you whole will make you stronger.

Re-entering the community requires risk, and risk is what collapse makes you allergic to. You want guarantees, assurance that if you step out, you will be embraced, not humiliated. But there are no guarantees. The first steps are always awkward. You show up at the meeting, the dinner, the gathering, with your past trailing behind you like a shadow. You speak up anyway. Each time you do, you prove to yourself that the past is not the only story you can tell.

One of the hardest parts of rebuilding in public is learning to contribute again. Collapse makes you self-absorbed. You spend months or years focused on your own shame, your own pain, your own survival. Reintegration into the community demands that you turn outward. You start asking not just "Who will accept me?" but "How can I serve here?" This shift is crucial. Service breaks the loop of self-absorption. It reminds you that you still have value to give, that you are not just a cautionary tale but a contributor.

I saw this truth watching survivors of natural disasters rebuild towns together. In Christchurch, New Zealand, after the earthquake, neighbors dug through rubble side by side. They didn't just clear debris; they cleared despair. Shared work turned survival into solidarity. That is what community can do: transform private grief into collective resilience.

Reinvention in the community also means becoming a builder yourself. The community you need may not exist yet. You might have to create it. I know people who started peer groups for others rebuilding after bankruptcy, after prison, after divorce, not as a performance of healing, but as a laboratory for honest conversation. Building a new community is slow, messy, and often lonely at first. But when it works, it gives you a place to stand that wasn't there before.

And here's the paradox: community will sometimes still judge you. They will misunderstand you. They will disappoint you. Reinvention doesn't mean finding a perfect tribe that never hurts you again. It means choosing to stay engaged anyway. It means choosing to risk belonging even when belonging feels dangerous.

Over time, the right community becomes a multiplier. It accelerates your growth, keeps you accountable, and refuses to let you settle for a version of yourself smaller than the one you are capable of becoming. This is why isolation is so dangerous, because alone, you will always be tempted to shrink.

Chapter 19 Exercise: The Circle Audit

Map Your Current Circles. Write down every community you are currently part of: work, family, friends, faith, and online groups.

Sort Them by Impact. Which ones expand you, and which ones shrink you? Which calls you to your best self, and which keep you bound to your worst chapter?

Choose One Act of Re-entry. Attend one gathering you've been avoiding. Volunteer once. Speak up once.

Choose One Act of Withdrawal. Step back from one space that keeps you trapped in old patterns. Silence a group chat. Say no to a gathering that drains you.

Repeat Monthly. Keep curating until the balance of your circles reflects the person you are becoming, not just the person you were.

Reinvention in the community is where the private work becomes visible. It is where the internal gains, clearing rubble, choosing fragments, and stacking small wins, turn into something that can support others. This is the moment when reinvention stops being just about you and becomes about building a world you want to belong to.

Chapter 20: Reinvention in Health

Health is the most silent part of reinvention until it stops being silent. When everything else in life collapses, you can ignore your body for a while. You can push through exhaustion, numb yourself with caffeine or alcohol, or pretend you'll "deal with it later." But collapse has a way of dragging health into the center of the stage, whether you want it there or not. The stress alone is corrosive, cortisol pumping day after day, sleep shredded, immune system shot. Collapse doesn't just wreck your plans. It wrecks your body.

I didn't notice it at first. I thought the exhaustion was just grief, that the headaches were from stress, that the weight gain was from comfort food and late nights. But over time, I realized collapse had turned my body into another kind of rubble. My digestion was a mess. My skin broke out. I woke at three a.m. every night, heart racing like I'd just sprinted. Reinvention had to include health, not as an afterthought, but as a cornerstone, or there would be nothing left to rebuild with.

This is the paradox: collapse strips away routines, but many of those routines were the only thing keeping you functional. Regular meals. Sleep cycles. Exercise. Once they vanish, the body begins to drift just like the mind does. You start skipping meals, or binging them. You stay up all night doom-scrolling. You forgot to drink water. You live on adrenaline until there's nothing left to burn.

The first act of health reinvention is not optimization. It's stabilization. Forget hacks and bio-hacks, supplements and cold plunges. The question is embarrassingly simple: Are you sleeping? Are you feeding yourself real food? Are you moving your body in some way every day? Reinvention begins by re-inhabiting your body, which is much harder than it sounds when you've been living in fight-or-flight for months.

For me, it started with sleep. Not perfect sleep, just an hour more than I had been getting. I began shutting screens off earlier, making the room darker, letting my nervous system downshift. That single act changed everything else. I had more patience. I stopped snapping at people. I could think again. From there, I began to walk. Just walk. No training program, no gym membership, just putting one foot in front of the other until the air started to feel like medicine instead of punishment.

Health reinvention is humbling because it refuses shortcuts. You can fake a confident smile. You can fake social belonging. You cannot fake bloodwork. You cannot fake the way your body crashes if you keep abusing it. Your cells are a feedback loop you cannot argue with.

History has shown that after crises, war, famine, and pandemics, societies rebuild health infrastructure first. Clean water. Food distribution. Shelter. Without those, nothing else stands. Personal reinvention works the same way. You can dream big visions for the future, but if you are running on fumes, those visions will never materialize.

Health is also where shame often hides. Collapse makes you want to punish yourself, and one of the easiest ways to punish yourself is by neglecting your body. You overwork it, underfeed it, flood it with junk, or numb it with substances. Part of reinvention is deciding you are worth caring for, not as a reward for success, but as a prerequisite for survival.

I knew a man who lost everything in a business scandal. For years afterward, he lived like his body was disposable, with fast food, heavy drinking, and no movement except to collapse into bed. It wasn't until he landed in the hospital with chest pain that he realized he had been compounding his collapse instead of climbing out of it. His reinvention began with quitting drinking, hiring a trainer, and learning to cook simple meals. He told me later: "I thought health would come last, once I had everything else figured out. Turns out it had to come first or nothing else would stick."

Health reinvention doesn't require perfection. It requires patterns. Small ones, repeated. A liter of water every morning. A bedtime you actually keep. Protein and vegetables most days rather than not. Movement that doesn't feel like punishment but like proof you are still here.

And it requires patience. The body does not reset overnight. It heals on its own timeline. You may feel worse at first, detoxing from years of neglect, facing the aches you've been ignoring. But just as small wins build momentum in life, small wins build momentum in health. The first good night of sleep. The first meal that leaves you feeling strong instead of sluggish. The first morning you wake up with real energy. These are as important as any business deal or relationship milestone.

When you treat your health as part of reinvention instead of an accessory to it, everything else becomes easier—your resilience increases. Your decision-making sharpens. Your emotions stop swinging so violently. The body and mind are not separate projects. They are the same project.

Chapter 20 Exercise: Health Baseline

Track the Basics. For one week, write down your hours of sleep, water intake, meals, and daily movement. Don't judge, just record.

Identify the Weakest Link. Which area is collapsing first: sleep, nutrition, movement, or stress management? Pick one.

Start with the Smallest Win. Choose a single, measurable habit. Go to bed 30 minutes earlier. Walk 10 minutes a day. Drink one more glass of water.

Stack Slowly. Add one habit each week until your baseline begins to feel stable.

Review Monthly. Ask yourself: Do I feel clearer, calmer, stronger? If not, adjust. Reinvention is not about pushing harder, but about supporting the system so it can hold.

Reinvention in health is not about becoming superhuman. It's about refusing to live as a ghost in your own body. It is about making the body a place where a new life can be carried, not just mentally, but physically.

Part VI: The Future.

Chapter 21: Anticipating Collapse

Collapse always feels sudden until it doesn't. People like to say, "no one saw it coming," but that's rarely true. Collapses leave footprints, small cracks, faint tremors, quiet warnings that most of us step over because we're too busy maintaining the illusion of control. The skill is not preventing collapse entirely, that's impossible, but learning to recognize its early signals before they turn into avalanches.

Anticipation is not paranoia. Paranoia keeps you frozen, scanning the horizon for threats until you forget to live. Anticipation is different. It is watchfulness. It is cultivating the discipline to read the room, to notice when the ground under your feet feels just slightly less solid than before, and to respond before the ice breaks.

When I look back at my own collapse, I see the warning signs everywhere. They weren't subtle. They just didn't fit the story I was telling myself, so I filtered them out. The conversations felt slightly off. The financial reports are instead of studying. The late-night anxiety that I drowned out with work or distraction. All of it was information, and I ignored it.

We are wired to do this. Our brains are prediction machines, and they crave coherence. When reality threatens the story we've been living, we tend to edit reality rather than rewrite the story. Psychologists call this confirmation bias, but in collapse, it becomes a kind of self-sabotage. We see what we want to see, until we can no longer.

Learning to anticipate collapse means reversing that reflex. Instead of avoiding dissonance, you lean into it. You treat every uncomfortable piece of data as a signal, not an annoyance. You ask: What is this trying to tell me? When you practice this long enough, it stops being catastrophic when the story breaks. You saw it coming. You've been preparing for it.

History is full of ignored warnings. The Challenger disaster came after engineers raised concerns about O-ring failure. The 2008 financial crisis followed years of experts warning about mortgage-backed securities. The Titanic received iceberg warnings on the very day it sank. The pattern is the same: someone sees the signs, but the system is too invested in the current story to stop. That's what makes anticipation so difficult; it is almost always inconvenient.

In my life, the first step toward anticipation was admitting that collapse is not rare. It's ordinary. Bodies fail. Markets crash. Trust erodes. The default state of the world is flux, not stability. Once you accept that, anticipating collapse stops feeling like pessimism and starts feeling like common sense.

The Three Horizons of Collapse

Over time, I've come to see three levels of collapse that we can learn to anticipate:

Micro-Collapses: The smallest failures, a missed deadline, a fight with a friend, a gut-level feeling that something is off. These are not disasters, but they are the smoke before the fire.

Structural Collapses: These happen when systems you rely on begin to weaken, a company bleeding cash, a relationship hollowing out, your own health degrading. These take longer to form, and they can be reversed if caught early.

Total Collapses: The full implosion, the business shuttered, the marriage dissolved, the diagnosis delivered, the reputation gone. These are the ones people call "sudden," but they are simply the final act of a much longer story.

Anticipation means scanning all three horizons regularly. It means asking hard questions before you are forced to. Where am I ignoring friction? Where am I coasting on luck instead of discipline? What am I afraid to look at?

The Courage to Look

Anticipation is an act of courage. Seeing a collapse coming doesn't protect you from grief; in some ways, it intensifies it, because you have to admit the loss before it becomes official. But courage on the front end saves you devastation on the back end. It buys you time to prepare, to plan, to soften the landing.

I remember sitting in my office three months before everything fell apart, staring at a spreadsheet that told me the truth. I closed the laptop and told myself I'd deal with it next week. I did that for twelve more weeks. When the crash finally came, I told myself it was sudden. It wasn't. It was my refusal to see what was already written.

Building an Anticipation Practice

Anticipation is not just awareness. It is a discipline. Here are three practices that changed how I relate to collapse:

Weekly Scan: Once a week, I write down every loose thread in my life, unpaid bills, strained conversations, unresolved conflicts, and strange gut feelings. Then I ask: if this unravels, what would it lead to? This habit has caught crises months before they became public.

Dissonance Journal: Whenever something feels off, I record it. Not to obsess over it, but to notice patterns. A single argument can be dismissed. A dozen arguments in a row are a trend.

Pre-Mortems: Before major projects or decisions, I ask: how could this fail? What would have to happen for this to collapse? Naming those scenarios in advance makes me less shocked if they occur, and sometimes prevents them altogether.

Anticipation is not about living in fear. It is about building the capacity to act early instead of late.

The Gift of Anticipation

The strange thing about learning to anticipate collapse is that it makes life calmer, not more anxious. When you stop pretending disaster is impossible, you stop being blindsided when it arrives. You stop bargaining with illusions. You stop defending what is already failing.

Instead, you begin to prepare exits, cultivate alternatives, and build relationships that can weather storms.

A friend of mine taught me this better than anyone. He lived through the 2008 crash, lost his house, and nearly lost his marriage. When he rebuilt, he swore never to be that exposed again. He keeps an emergency fund, an updated resume, and a running list of people he can call if work dries up. Not because he expects disaster tomorrow, but because he knows it will come eventually. He sleeps better now, not worse.

The Choice

Collapse is inevitable. The question is whether you let it blindside you or whether you meet it halfway. You cannot prevent every fall, but you can train yourself to notice when the ground shifts, to listen when your gut warns you, to act when the story no longer fits reality.

Anticipation does not remove the pain of collapse. But it does transform the meaning. Collapse stops being a violent ambush and becomes a hard but honest teacher.

Chapter 21 Exercise: Collapse Pre-Mortem

Take out a sheet of paper and write down the three most important areas of your life right now: work, relationships, and health. For each, answer these questions:

What is the most likely way this could collapse?

What signs would I see three months before that collapse?

What could I do now to reduce the impact if it happened?

When you finish, circle one small preventive action and take it this week. It doesn't have to be dramatic, a conversation, a check-up, or a review of finances. The point is not to predict perfectly but to break the habit of blindness.

Collapse will come again. That's not fatalism, that's reality. But once you learn to anticipate it, you stop being defined by it. You stop treating it as an ending and start treating it as part of the rhythm of a life that is constantly breaking and remaking itself.

Chapter 22: Reinvention as Foresight

Reinvention is not just about recovering from collapse. It is about living in such a way that collapse is no longer the only teacher. You cannot erase instability from life; it is built into the system, but you can stop being blindsided by it. The highest form of reinvention is foresight: building lives, systems, and habits that anticipate failure, absorb shock, and turn volatility into raw material for growth.

At first, foresight feels like paranoia. After you've lived through a collapse, your mind becomes hypervigilant, scanning every horizon for danger. The risk is overcorrecting, becoming so cautious that you never try again. But foresight is not fear; it is preparation without panic. It is the discipline of seeing reality as it is, not as you wish it to be, and making choices today that make tomorrow survivable.

When I first started to rebuild, I made the mistake of thinking reinvention was just about cleaning up the wreckage. I wanted to fix the past, to prove that I could return to the same life, only better. But that was just nostalgia wearing a mask. Real reinvention doesn't just rebuild the old house. It redesigns the architecture, so the next storm doesn't knock it down in the same way.

Foresight begins with pattern recognition. Every collapse leaves a map of its origins, ignored warnings, overconfidence, and unsustainable pressure. If you study those patterns closely, you start to see echoes of them in the present. You notice when ambition is driving you past your own limits. You hear the silence in a relationship as a signal, not an afterthought. You catch yourself before you drift back into shortcuts and rationalizations.

The shift is subtle but profound: instead of living reactively, you begin living pre-emptively. You prepare for the next collapse, not because you are pessimistic but because you accept reality. This is how resilient cultures operate. Japan builds earthquake-resistant homes not because it believes the ground will never shake again, but because it knows it will. Pilots train for engine failure, not because they expect to crash every flight, but because they refuse to be surprised when something goes wrong.

I had to learn to design my life with similar redundancies. I stopped tying my entire identity to one role, one business, one source of meaning. I diversified my sources of stability. I built financial buffers where I once lived on the edge. I cultivated relationships that could withstand truth instead of just comfort. I built habits that kept me grounded: reflection, journaling, and check-ins with friends who weren't afraid to call me out. These weren't glamorous gestures. They were quiet, unglamorous investments in a future self I hadn't met yet.

Foresight also means learning to read the weather of your own mind. Collapse does not only come from external events, but it also comes from inner erosion. The burnout you ignore, the bitterness you feed, the resentment you rehearse, these are fault lines. Left unattended, they widen. Reinvention as foresight means tending to them early. It means having hard conversations before silence becomes permanent, stepping back before exhaustion becomes collapse, seeking help before pride convinces you you're fine.

This is not just self-preservation. It is a strategy. When you live with foresight, you stop playing defense and start designing the game. You build systems that are shock absorbers instead of brittle glass. You make decisions with optionality in mind, leaving yourself multiple exits, multiple ways to pivot if things go wrong.

The paradox is that this kind of preparation doesn't make you anxious; it makes you freer. Once you've accepted that collapse is inevitable, you stop clinging to illusions. You stop gripping your plans with white knuckles. You begin to hold things lightly, ready to release them if necessary, confident that you will rebuild again if you must.

Foresight turns reinvention from a one-time event into a posture, a way of inhabiting time. You stop waiting for catastrophe to tell you what matters. You decide what matters now, and you start living as though the clock is already ticking, because it is.

Chapter 22 Exercise: Designing for the Next Collapse

Take out a sheet of paper and draw three columns labeled "Likely Failures," "Early Warning Signs," and "My Response."

In the first column, list the most likely collapses you could face in the next five years: losing a job, facing illness, a relationship ending, or a financial downturn.

In the second column, write the signals that would tell you the collapse is coming: performance reviews slipping, chronic fatigue, constant conflict, and rising debt.

In the third column, write one action you could take today to make that collapse survivable: update your resume, schedule a health screening, initiate a conversation, or create a savings plan.

This practice is not about trying to outsmart life or eliminate risk. It is about refusing to be caught unaware. It is about becoming the kind of person who is ready, not because disaster is fun, but because you have decided that collapse will no longer be the thing that determines who you are.

Reinvention as foresight is the graduate level of this work. It is the refusal to keep learning the same lesson by living through the same pain. It is the choice to break the cycle, to face reality early, and to keep moving forward even as you hear the ice cracking beneath your feet.

Chapter 23: Teaching Reinvention

At some point, reinvention stops being only about you. The ground you've cleared, the fragments you've chosen, the momentum you've built — they are not just for your benefit. They are raw material for others. People are always watching, even if they don't say so. Some are looking for proof that survival is possible. Others are waiting to see if you will stay down. Whether you like it or not, your reinvention is a lesson — the only question is whether you teach it on purpose.

I once met a man whose son had been arrested for a crime eerily similar to one he himself had committed decades earlier. The father admitted he had never told his son the full story of his own collapse, never shared how far he had fallen, never described the years it took to rebuild. "I didn't want him to think less of me," he said. The son learned the lesson anyway, but he knew it by living it — paying with years of his own life. Silence doesn't protect. It leaves the people around you unarmed.

Teaching reinvention is not standing on a soapbox shouting your triumphs. It is telling the truth about the wreckage and the slow climb out — without editing out the failures, without polishing the lessons so they shine like cheap inspiration posters. It is sharing the story honestly so that someone else can see the terrain before they walk into it.

The temptation, especially once you've begun to recover, is to turn your pain into performance. We've all seen the redemption monologues – the big speech about "lessons learned" that plays well at conferences and dinner parties but rings hollow to the people who were actually hurt. Teaching reinvention is not an audition for forgiveness. It is a form of service. You teach because you know what it feels like to go blind in the dark. You teach so that someone else can light a match.

Witness → Translate → Offer

The first step in teaching reinvention is witnessing your own journey honestly. If you lie to yourself about what happened, you will lie to others. Name the collapse in detail. Remember what it cost you. Acknowledge the parts you caused and the parts that were simply fate. Your story is not useful until you stop trying to make yourself the hero.

The second step is translation. Most people can't use your exact story. They need to know what it means, not just what it looked like. Translate the raw events into principles they can apply. If your business failed because you ignored cash flow, the principle is not "don't start a business" — it's "watch your liquidity before it strangles you." If your marriage fell apart because you avoided hard conversations, the principle isn't "don't marry" — it's "speak before silence becomes permanent." Translation turns autobiography into usable instruction.

The final step is offering. You cannot force your lessons on anyone. People take what they're ready for and leave the rest. The offer is not a lecture but an open hand: "Here's what I learned. Take it if it's useful." Some will ignore you. Some will laugh. A few will listen. Those few make it worth the risk.

The Cost of Not Teaching

I've seen what happens when people refuse to pass on what they've learned. They repeat the same collapse, generation after generation. Families that never talk about money see bankruptcy play out like clockwork. Parents who never admit their addictions watch their children stumble into the same traps. Companies that bury their failures under PR spin collapse again under the same pressures. What you refuse to teach, life will teach — but at a far higher cost.

Your story doesn't have to be public to matter. Some of the most powerful acts of teaching happen in kitchens, over coffee, in quiet moments when someone younger than you asks, "What would you do differently?" You can give them an answer that might save them years — if you're brave enough to speak plainly.

The Fear of Being Seen

Teaching reinvention is terrifying because it means telling the truth about who you were at your worst. I hesitated for years, convinced that if I spoke honestly about my collapse, people would use it against me. And some did. But others came closer, not further away. They said, "I thought I was the only one." They said, "Your story gave me the courage to stop lying." Teaching doesn't just help others. It redeems your pain by turning it into something useful.

The paradox is that by exposing the mess, you actually earn more credibility. People are not inspired by perfection — they are inspired by survival. They trust those who have been to the bottom and are still standing.

Chapter 23 Exercise: The Lesson Ledger

Take a sheet of paper and divide it into three columns:

What Happened: Write three moments from your collapse that changed you. Be specific and unflinching.

What It Taught Me: Write the principle or insight that came from each moment. Avoid clichés. Name the lesson in a way that you would have needed to hear it.

Who Needs It: Write the name of someone — a friend, a younger colleague, a family member — who might need that lesson now.

Choose one person and share one lesson in the next week. You don't have to stage a dramatic intervention. A text, a phone call, or a short conversation will do. The point is to stop hoarding what you've learned and begin putting it into circulation.

Teaching reinvention is not the final chapter. It is the multiplier. Your story becomes more than a private recovery project; it becomes part of someone else's survival kit. Collapse took enough from you. Don't let it take the wisdom too. Pass it on.

Chapter 24: Reinvention Without End

Every collapse in this book has been leading here: to the truth that nothing lasts. Work ends. Health falters. Relationships change. Communities fracture. Identities dissolve. Collapse is not an interruption to life — it is the architecture of life itself. And because collapse is inevitable, reinvention must be continual. Reinvention is not a single act of recovery; it is the permanent rhythm of survival.

This truth can feel cruel at first. We are wired to long for stability, to dream of arrival points where struggle ends and permanence begins. We build careers, marriages, nations, and religions in the hope that something will finally hold. Collapse shatters that illusion again and again. If you cling to permanence, every loss feels like betrayal. If you accept impermanence, collapse feels less like tragedy and more like confirmation: the cycle is still turning. Everything ends, so the work is always to begin again.

I resisted this truth for years. After each collapse, I swore this would be the last one. Once I rebuilt, I thought I'd be safe, insulated from the next fall. But safety never came. Another collapse always followed. At first, this felt like punishment, like the universe was conspiring to keep me from peace. Later, I understood: collapse wasn't punishment, it was a pattern. Reinvention wasn't a phase to graduate from. It was the shape my life had to take if I wanted to keep living at all.

History is clear on this point. Every empire that declared itself eternal eventually fell. Every civilization that believed it had transcended fragility was humbled. Humanity has endured not because we prevented collapse but because we reinvented — again and again — when collapse came. The story of humanity is not one of permanence. It is the story of relentless renewal.

The same is true on the smallest, most personal scale. Your body will fail, piece by piece, no matter how carefully you tend it. Your closest relationships will change shape no matter how loyal you are. Your work will end no matter how excellent you become. If you measure life by stability, despair is inevitable. If you measure it by reinvention, you can keep going.

And here is the paradox: when you stop demanding that life stay the same, it stops feeling so heavy. When you stop being shocked by endings, you start living more lightly. You love more honestly because you know bonds are fragile. You work with more freedom because you know careers are temporary. You are more present in your own body because you know health is fleeting. Reinvention without end is not despair. It is liberation.

I once sat with an older man who had survived war, famine, migration, illness, and unbearable personal loss. I asked him how he kept starting over. He smiled — not bitterly, but with a quiet peace — and said, "You think life is about keeping what you have. It isn't. Life is about starting again, over and over, until you can't anymore. That's all it is."

The lesson was simple, but it stayed with me. The point was never to reach a plateau where reinvention stops. The fact is to become practiced at beginning again, so that each new collapse finds you less afraid. Collapse will always sit on your shoulder, whispering its presence. But when you accept reinvention as your permanent companion, the whisper stops sounding like a threat. It becomes a rhythm you know by heart.

Chapter 24 Exercise: Embracing Endless Reinvention

Name Your Myth of Arrival. Write down the fantasy you've been holding — the day when everything will be safe, finished, unbreakable.

Tear It Down. List three reasons why that fantasy cannot exist: collapse will return, change is inevitable, and identity will keep shifting.

Reframe It. Write: *Reinvention is not a phase. It is my practice.* Sit with it until it feels less like a punishment and more like permission.

Design Your Rhythm. Choose one ritual to remind you that reinvention is ongoing — a seasonal reset, an annual reflection, a monthly check-in. Let it anchor you.

Name Your Ripple. Write one way your practice of reinvention could ripple outward to others. Let that ripple give your work meaning beyond your own survival.

Reinvention without end is not a sentence — it is freedom from illusion. You no longer need to chase the fantasy of permanence or fear its collapse. You no longer need to panic when the ground shifts. Reinvention becomes less of an emergency and more of a posture, the way you meet every ending, every loss, every beginning. This is the last lesson and the first one: collapse will come, and when it does, you will start again.

Epilogue: Reinvention as Legacy

Reinvention was never just about you. The work you have done — clearing the rubble, choosing what to keep, stacking small wins, anticipating the next collapse — has already started to ripple outward. People who know you have been watching. Some are rooting for you. Some are waiting to see if you fail. And a few are quietly wondering if what you've done is possible for them.

Legacy is not what you leave behind when you die. Legacy is the shape your life is carving right now. Every choice you make becomes a signal. Every time you rise again, you make survival visible to someone who thought they were done.

Reinvention as legacy is not loud. It doesn't need to be. You do not have to write a book, give a speech, or start a movement. Sometimes your presence is enough. Sometimes the most radical thing you can offer is to keep showing up, day after day, living proof that collapse is not the end.

When I look back on the people who kept me alive when I was at my lowest, most of them didn't say much. They stayed. They didn't rush me, didn't demand I be cheerful or productive or "positive." Their quiet steadiness told me

I wasn't finished, even when I believed I was. That is what legacy looks like: showing others by your own life that starting again is possible.

Collapse will visit you again. It will see the people you love. When it does, the work you've done will be a kind of map – not to spare them the pain, but to give them a way through it. This is why you keep going, not just for yourself, but for the people who will need proof that the world is still survivable.

Legacy isn't measured in monuments. It's measured in courage. Every time you start again, you leave behind a pattern others can follow. That pattern might just be the thing that saves them.

Epilogue Exercise: Leaving a Reinvention Map

Take a blank page and write down three things you wish someone had told you before your collapse – the truths you had to learn the hard way. Then choose one of the following ways to share them:

One-on-one: Tell someone in your circle who might need it – a friend, a child, a colleague.

Write it down: Capture it in a letter, journal, or even a short post. Not for attention, but so it exists outside your head.

Model it: Choose one action this week that embodies what you've learned — generosity, honesty, patience — and let someone see you do it.

This small act becomes a marker, a quiet breadcrumb left behind for anyone who will one day need to follow the path you've already walked.

About The Author

Rowan Blake is a writer, strategist, and quiet rebel in the world of digital culture. With a background in media, design, and systems thinking, Rowan explores how modern creators can navigate visibility without losing their voice. Their work focuses on the intersection of technology and humanity, how algorithms shape behavior, how attention is captured and spent, and what it takes to stay grounded in a landscape that rarely stops moving.

Rowan writes for creators, entrepreneurs, and curious minds who care less about chasing trends and more about building something real. With a style that's reflective, sharp, and deeply personal, Rowan's books and essays help readers rethink the cost of constant optimization and imagine more sustainable, meaningful ways to create and connect.

This is Rowan's second book in The Book On Series. It comes after her successful debut book, Mastering the Algorithm.

Outside of writing, Rowan consults for values-driven startups, reads everything from neuroscience to speculative fiction, and occasionally disappears offline to recalibrate.

About The Publisher

Welcome to The Book On Publishing

At The Book On Publishing, we believe in rewriting the rules of learning. Whether you're chasing your next big idea, building a better life, or simply curious about what should have been taught in school, you've come to the right place.

We're a platform built for dreamers, doers, and lifelong learners, offering bold, practical books and tools that empower you to take charge of your journey. From real-world skills to mindset mastery, we publish the book on what matters.

No fluff. No lectures. Just what you need to know, delivered with clarity, purpose, and a spark of curiosity.

Start exploring. Start growing. Start writing your story.

Read more at https://thebookon.ca.

Acknowledgment of AI Assistance

Portions of this book were developed with the support of AI. While every word has been carefully reviewed and refined by the author, AI served as a valuable tool for brainstorming, editing, and structuring ideas. Its assistance helped accelerate the creative process and bring clarity to complex topics.